TRAUMA AND RENEWAL

TRAUMA AND RENEWAL

Toward Spiritual, Communal, and Holistic Transformation

Aizaiah G. Yong

with contributions from Amos and Alma Yong

ORBIS BOOKS
Maryknoll, New York 10545

Founded in 1970, Orbis Books endeavors to publish works that enlighten the mind, nourish the spirit, and challenge the conscience. The publishing arm of the Maryknoll Fathers and Brothers, Orbis seeks to explore the global dimensions of the Christian faith and mission, to invite dialogue with diverse cultures and religious traditions, and to serve the cause of reconciliation and peace. The books published reflect the views of their authors and do not represent the official position of the Maryknoll Society. To learn more about Maryknoll and Orbis Books, please visit our website at www.orbisbooks.com.

Copyright © 2025 by Aizaiah G. Yong

Published by Orbis Books, Box 302, Maryknoll, NY 10545-0302.

All rights reserved.

No part of this publication may be reproduced or transmitted in any form or by any means, electronic or mechanical, including photocopying, recording, or any information storage or retrieval system, without prior permission in writing from the publisher.

Queries regarding rights and permissions should be addressed to: Orbis Books, P.O. Box 302, Maryknoll, NY 10545-0302.

Scripture quotations are taken from the New Revised Standard Version Updated Edition. Copyright © 2021 National Council of Churches of Christ in the United States of America. Used by permission. All rights reserved worldwide.

Manufactured in the United States of America

Library of Congress Cataloging-in-Publication Data

Names: Yong, Aizaiah G., author. | Yong, Amos, author. | Yong, Alma, author.
Title: Trauma and renewal : toward spiritual, communal, and holistic transformation / Aizaiah G. Yong with contributions from Amos and Alma Yong.
Description: Maryknoll, New York : Orbis Books, [2025] | Includes bibliographical references. | Summary: "A spiritual, holistic, and community-based approach to trauma healing"— Provided by publisher.
Identifiers: LCCN 2024057134 (print) | LCCN 2024057135 (ebook) | ISBN 9781626986190 (trade paperback) | ISBN 9798888660744 (epub)
Subjects: LCSH: Spiritual healing. | Well-being—Religious aspects—Christianity.
Classification: LCC BT732.5 .Y66 2025 (print) | LCC BT732.5 (ebook) | DDC 234/.131—dc23/eng/20241231
LC record available at https://lccn.loc.gov/2024057134
LC ebook record available at https://lccn.loc.gov/2024057135

To my Yong, Ti, Garcia, and Rios Ancestors past, present, and future.

Thank you for all you have taught me about wholeness, healing, and liberation.

May the lessons I have received be shared unto the world for the sake of

all-encompassing renewal, flourishing, and transformation.

"It is the responsibility of free men to trust and to celebrate what is constant—birth, struggle, and death are constant, and so is love, though we may not always think so—and to apprehend the nature of change, to be able and willing to change. I speak of change not on the surface but in the depths—change in the sense of renewal."

—James Baldwin

CONTENTS

Introduction: Yearning for Wholeness 1

PART I: WITNESS

   1. Unknowing 27

   2. With-ness-ing 46

   3. Befriending the Tears 61

PART II: VISIONS

   4. Radiating Love. 79

   5. Experiencing Aliveness. 102

   6. Every Being Belongs 116

PART III: LIBERATIVE COMMUNITY

   7. Seeing One Another. 133

   8. Expanding Companionship 153

   9. Rising Again ... and Again. 168

Afterword: Wholeness Is Not a One-Time Event. 177

Acknowledgments. 180

Notes. 183

vii

INTRODUCTION

Yearning for Wholeness

One moment can change a life forever. For me, that moment occurred on October 16, 2018, when I endured a dramatic and life-changing accident. To this day I still suffer from chronic physical disability as I continue down the long road of trauma recovery.

Often the journey has felt isolating, overwhelming, and discouraging, but what I have learned is that it is crushing when the journey is attempted alone. The book you are now holding is not only a book about my experience but a spiritual and communal reflection on trauma, concerned with how we pursue wholeness in deep relationship with others. Maybe you picked up this book because you survived a serious traumatic event yourself or perhaps you wonder how to best show up and support others who have experienced trauma. Either way, I hope you'll agree that the time is ripe to ask new questions about trauma and transformation in the hope we'll be led to new possibilities of personal and collective healing. Together we will ask questions that move us beyond individualism without losing the sense of the

Trauma and Renewal

personal and explore questions that move us beyond well-dressed and sanitized explanations of trauma while moving toward hope that can guide our actions in the now and for the future.

In my work over the last decade as a clergy person, psychospiritual practitioner, and interreligious educator, I have witnessed traumas great and small. From individual and acute trauma to complex and chronic trauma to systemic and intergenerational trauma. While each of these has important distinctions, what unites them is the yearning in those who've faced trauma to be restored to wholeness. Wherever you may be on your journey, I trust you will find you are not alone in your pursuit of wholeness and that you will be inspired to uncover inner wisdom along the way.

Like many others affected by trauma, I have been on a quest toward wholeness for quite some time. I've looked far and wide and often found myself doubting if deeper healing was even possible. What I've discovered is that there isn't one magical recipe toward wholeness, but rather an ever-unfolding awareness and practice of relating to all that is within me and beyond me with compassion that moves me toward a greater sense of wholeness. That is why, for me, trauma transformation is profoundly relational. Many I'll name in this book were gracious in accompanying me in my ongoing healing journey. But I want to especially acknowledge my father, Amos Yong, and my mother, Alma Yong, who both experienced secondary trauma through the events and

Introduction

aftermath of my ordeal. They also were the ones who became my two primary caretakers during the approximately half-year period when I was unable to eat, bathe, or walk on my own. While the effects of trauma can linger for a lifetime, this book aims to tell a different story: the story about the relational ways we are called to continually support each other when the inescapable happens and amid the continuing transformations that unfold in our lives. This book seeks to offer and call forth spiritual, communal, and intercultural paradigms of trauma transformation because as we continue to discover, the only way forward is together.

At its core, this book offers three primary convictions, which I invite you to explore with me:

1. How spiritual narratives and story-sharing can be tools of empowerment in the aftermath of trauma, especially for those in marginalized communities whose experiences are consistently dismissed by forces of social oppression.
2. How contemplative spiritualities offer a distinct approach to the work of trauma transformation because they are experiential, holistic, and creative.
3. How contemporary psychospiritual models of healing (primarily Internal Family Systems [IFS], in which I have been trained as a level-two practitioner) have a lot to teach us about tending to trauma somatically.

Trauma and Renewal

While I hope the convictions above may resonate with you, even if they do not, I invite you to simply practice curiosity with yourself as you read, noticing what moves you.

The stories or principles I share may bring you joy, tears, consolation, or even emotional activation. Of utmost importance, though, is to move through your own journey of trauma transformation slowly, being patient with the process, and extending self-compassion toward the most vulnerable parts inside of yourself.

If you are like me, extending self-compassion is easier said than done. And you may find yourself being harsh or critical toward your experience; you are not alone in this. And so, I want to offer you a few gentle practices intended to ease your process with the material:

- Find a sacred space to read the book. A sacred space means something different for each of us, but it could involve grounding sights (images, icons), sounds (running water), or smells (aromatic candles) in the physical room you are in, or finding a relaxing place in nature that supports a sense of centeredness.
- Avoid rushing or hurrying as you engage the material. When we're activated or stirred up inside, it is tempting to speed things up and hope the discomfort will pass. But when it comes to healing, each of our activations has a lot to teach us. It is essential we don't dismiss, ignore, or push strong

Introduction

activation away, but rather slow things down, reground, and see if we can become curious about what is arising for us. If the activation becomes a bit too much, seeking professional mental health support that is also culturally sensitive is crucial.

- Reflect personally on the shared stories. While the exact details of my journey will differ from yours, I invite you to explore what comes up within you personally as you read. Ask yourself, is there resonance in my own story? Are there threads of personal connection? How is my story or experience different? When asking these questions and responding, it can be helpful to either journal or audio-record your own voice sharing what's coming up for you, and really allowing yourself time to partake in and digest what is being offered. After you have taken some time with the material, I encourage you to identify what is life affirming for you where you are in your own journey—and you'll know it as such because of the way it arises from within you as a knowing and longing toward new possibilities of experiencing wholeness.

- Share your journey with others while exercising prudence and discernment. I do not recommend a public broadcast of one's suffering, especially when it has not been processed in a space that is supportive and judgment free. Yet it is so important to find trusted people whom you can share your lived experiences with. Individual reflection alone is not sufficient for a fulfilling human experience, and I have found that so much of what we long for is transformed in the sharing itself. We long to tell our stories, be seen, felt, and known by others. And one of the ways toward this intimacy is to share aspects of our story with those who will keep confidentiality, honor our story, and treat us with dignity and respect.

MY STORY OF TRAUMA TRANSFORMATION

Initially, I hesitated to write a book about my personal experience with trauma. I thought, *does the world really need another book on trauma and spirituality?* But in many ways this book was being written long before I followed the encouragement of many friends (who are also spiritual care professionals) to make this public. Only days after the accident I began journaling, and I have returned to many of those entries throughout the process of writing this book, allowing the layers of my experience to deepen and provide windows for further integration.

I have also been through many years of personal therapy, psychospiritual training, and healing sessions of various kinds, including nature-based work, ancestral healing, and somatic meditation. Even with a great commitment to ongoing personal work, what I have learned is that writing and journaling is a profoundly spiritual practice for me. Writing supports me in

Introduction

expressing and transforming the raw feelings deep within. And through this process, I am invited to look more fully at my lived experience and called to grow in patience, mercy, and compassion. My hope is that in reading this book and perhaps writing or discovering a means for your own ever-deepening reflection, you will also experience a greater freedom and awareness of the personal experiences you have lived and how that can be offered back unto the world for collective liberation.

Given that this book dives into my own story, it is important for me to share with readers the context of my story and my social location. It's important to preface many facets of my identity, including among other things, my cisgender maleness, physical disability, middle socioeconomic status, my profession as a professor, and my ordination as a self-identifying Pentecostal minister in a mainline Protestant Christian denomination in North America.

Each of these aspects of my experience informs how I move in the world, and it is especially important for me to add specifically a focus on my multiethnic, multiracial, and second-generation immigrant experience. As somebody who has spent a great deal of time writing, teaching, and educating others on antiracism in the North American context, I find it's critical to reflect on our racialized experiences and interrogate how race influences multiple dimensions of our lives,[1] including trauma.

I am racialized as a mixed-race person of color. Ethnically my father is Chinese–Malaysian, and my mother is

Trauma and Renewal

Mexican–American, so I grew up in a household where multiple languages, traditions, and understandings of love coexisted. And it was in this upbringing where I learned about the joys of filial piety, *mi gente,* and the challenges that come from generational struggles with poverty, racism, and white Christian supremacy. It was also in this household that I learned about the ways in which spirituality can become a way of empowerment guiding us toward healing, creative action, and courage to resist oppression. I name these multi-dimensional aspects of my experience to show that tending trauma holistically requires that we become aware of our full embodied selves, making connections with the many pieces of our stories so often left behind.

What has been unique about my own process of writing a memoir related to my journey with and after trauma is that my story brings in the active and collaborative voice of primary caregivers who walked with me through my traumatic experience. Mostly in this book you'll hear the voice of my father, Amos Yong, also a theologian, but, in addition, there will be short essential reflections from mother, Alma Yong. You'll discover as you read that this book assumes the interconnectedness of both primary and secondary experiences of trauma, even as it entertains creative possibilities for transforming trauma when approached in community with others who are open and available.

Community healing, of course, is not a given since many firsthand and secondhand trauma survivors

Introduction

feel ill-equipped to return to the suffering, not least because of the presence of legacies of oppression and the ways dominant cultures perpetuate the stigmatization of suffering. In addition, transforming trauma in community requires a great deal of personal consent and willingness to embark upon inner transformation from each party involved, something not every person is open to. Yet, even with the many challenges to tending trauma in community, we can discover that when there is a willingness, a greater and more expansive restoration becomes possible. And while my voice is predominant and informed by my practical theological and psychospiritual training, every word that has been written has been shared with and transformed by ongoing dialogue with my parents so that together we could seek a greater sense of wholeness. In this respect, you may find this is a different approach from other books related to memoir, trauma healing, and spiritual care. It is an intergenerational and poly-vocal account embracing the central role of spirituality in trauma transformation.

A spiritual memoir of this kind allows a person to identify personal, familial, cultural, and intergenerational wisdom buried beneath the surface of dominant narratives within North American society (which center on individualism, reductionism, and materialism) and provide alternative imaginations for what makes us whole. As we will discover, trauma transformation is not just about physical or emotional care but calls us to make amends with cultural and intergenerational

Trauma and Renewal

legacies that have been handed down to us. To that end, this book assumes that our unique and specific cultural backgrounds have a lot to reveal about how we suffer and the diverse paths we take toward wholeness.

In the North American context, traditional trauma treatments have historically been individualistic, monocultural, and Eurocentric. But there are other approaches and insights for tending to trauma that come from the experiences of the global majority. Together we are invited to retrieve cultural heirlooms that perhaps were denied or delegitimized due to forces of oppression.

Despite (or perhaps due to) my predominantly North American and Christian-based theological training, I see it as imperative to rediscover the spiritual paradigms that come from traditions across the global majority long excluded from consideration. For example, while various streams within the Abrahamic traditions center trauma and suffering as a focal point of the human story and look to resolve it eschatologically, many Indigenous and East Asian cultures do not focus on trauma in any sustained way, but rather emphasize creativity, interdependence, and relationality at the core of experience.

Connected to the ethnic identity I inherited, as a Chinese–Malaysian–Mexican–American, there are spiritualities I've chosen to incorporate. This book looks at three East Asian spiritualities: Confucianism, Buddhism, and Daoism, and two examples, the Taki Oncoy and the Coyolxauhqui, from Latin American Indigenous spiritualities. I do not speak on behalf of (nor authoritatively

Introduction

on) any of the traditions listed above, as there is great diversity within each. Yet I turn to them in personal engagement and reflection.

With Confucianism, we dive into the premise that if one is to change the world, we must first seek to transform the most intimate relations around us. In Buddhism, we explore how wisdom is exemplified by a movement toward the acceptance and alleviation of suffering rather than an avoidance, and we also look to the example of Guanyin, the goddess of compassion. In Daoism, we turn to the wisdom of the Yin and Yang symbol, which represents a harmony and creative engagement with the polarities inherent to reality and, specifically as it relates to trauma, the polarity of joy and suffering. With the Taki Oncoy resistance movement, we open ourselves to the wisdom that comes from collective responses to injustice. And finally, the symbol of the Coyolxauhqui reminds us to bring the various fragments of our experience into creative relationship. We look to these cultural perspectives to reposition us in our relationship to trauma and to offer us alternatives about how we tend to it. This book invites each of us to consider other paradigms and models when it comes to tending trauma and committing a life to the long haul of the work of intercultural healing and collective liberation.

Contemporary trauma workers range in their focus: personal, collective, intergenerational, and ecological. And while each has unique and important contributions to the whole, all are in accord in recognizing that

Trauma and Renewal

we are living through times of massive displacement, collective trauma, and increasing fragmentation. Wars and genocide, political discord, ecological degradation, economic greed, and religious pride all feed narratives of self-preservation and tribal survival that breed an *us versus them* mentality. And while the atrocities are evil in themselves, our responses are hindered by our inability to tend trauma skillfully. In the age of information and instant news, we become paralyzed with the loads of suffering and "doomscroll," filling our minds with sensationalist reports of mass death, heightening our fear, and increasing our anxiety about the future. The cycle rages on and debilitates our capacity for creative action. We desperately need alternative approaches.

From modern psychology we know that trauma is not a simple one-time event. There are layers to trauma that live within ourselves, and thus the work requires devotion and commitment. James Finley, a psychologist and spiritual director for over four decades, describes the power of relationality in healing as the basis of the quickening occurring when you risk sharing what hurts the most with others without fear of being invaded or abandoned. Finley acknowledges this is easier said than done and is a delicate act to live out, one that requires great humility, trust, and openness.

Finley goes on to advise all those seeking to accompany others who are traumatized that, "one must keep a foot in being present and the other in their circle of suffering as a way of staying grounded in that

Introduction

which transcends the suffering."[2] "Being present" for Finley is both an *awareness of* and *trust in* the spiritual foundations of reality itself. And so, while there are particular skills that are important to learn when providing companionship to others, all those skills can be greatly strengthened through personal awareness of and connection with the sacred. *The sacred* here does not necessarily mean a belief in a deity or even a higher power, but rather an awareness and acknowledgment of interconnectedness with all things. For Finley, our healing must involve the sacred dimensions of our experience and need not only occur in therapeutic settings but also begin and sometimes deepen through intimate friendships and peer relationships in community.

It is important to name the relational possibilities of trauma transformation because this demonstrates how we value and identify community-based responses. Our predominant models of trauma care rely primarily on one-on-one approaches that are inaccessible and undesirable to many different people due to cost, culture, or a mixture of the two. Communities that have been historically marginalized suffer even more so without the privilege of time, economic resources, or a just medical system. But that does not mean there are no healing options available. In this book, we will explore the potential of incorporating psychospiritual skills alongside culturally based healing practices and philosophies, taking a both/and approach. I aim to affirm aspects of contemporary psychospiritual models of transformation

Trauma and Renewal

and bring those into conversation with cultural practices from the global majority for the purposes of imagining emergent modes of healing that are relational, intercultural, and based in mutuality rather than those based in the "expert–nonexpert" paradigm.

So how are we to articulate our current challenges with greater precision so our communities can flourish? And what skills and paradigms are helpful as we find our way through supporting one another? Our work is vital because at some point or another, we will all need care from others and likely it will be diverse others who we find ourselves in community with. Disability activists and abolitionist practitioners have long pointed this out, demonstrating how the lines between caregiver and the care receiver are blurred and can often interchange case by case and from situation to situation. Our ever-changing dynamics of care require new models of practice that center cultural diversity, belonging for the most vulnerable, and are imbued with a sense of the sacred. Access to health care for all is certainly important and desirable, but more money and material resources alone will not assure the transformation of our traumas—we must undergo a deep change of consciousness and awaken to the transformative capacities that lay dormant within.

When it comes to contemporary healing models, we see a clear call for trauma companions to assume a posture of compassion, care, and curiosity. Studies have shown how important it is for trauma companions to

Introduction

be grounded, open hearted, and present when working with severe trauma because even without saying a word, the very embodied reality of a calm person can create space for healing in another. Examples of this possibility can be found in the ideas of co-regulation (rather than self-regulation) and attachment theory. All too often our healing practices focus only on the therapist–client relationship, but what happens if we begin to embody these skills in our everyday wider community that also embraces our unique cultural wisdoms? I am not suggesting that we all become therapists, but rather that we collectively grow our skills of working with trauma.

Thankfully there is a growing number of psychospiritual models that wed the psychological sciences with a sense of spiritual wisdom. One such example that this book finds grounding in is the model of Internal Family Systems (IFS). As a level-two trained IFS practitioner, I have come to see how truth is not exhausted in any single person or experience but contains many dimensions to it and that we can discover those multiple dimensions through connection with "the Self." According to IFS, the Self is a primordial source of wisdom within each person that is inherently restorative and does not impose itself but remains available, even if hidden underneath the layers of suffering the person endures. And the key to IFS is to practice connection with the Self: within, with others, and in the world at large.

Trauma and Renewal

Thanks to its understanding of the Self, IFS teaches a way of tending trauma that is a radically nonpathologizing and compassionate approach toward embracing the suffering parts of the psyche, contending that there is much wisdom to be integrated from them. In my work with the IFS model for the past five years, I have practiced it personally, interpersonally, and I have explored it as a collective practice in religion-based settings among those with diverging multiple spiritual, cultural, or religious identities. I regularly turn to principles and practices of IFS to help encourage relational approaches to trauma transformation. Because transforming trauma is not a quick-fix approach, but rather a deeply implicating and relational process, it calls for perseverance, tenderness, and a willingness to hold the hurting places of life with fierce gentleness. While trauma theologies are now wedding together with narrative studies and the psychological sciences, this book will also build upon them and add the practiced dimensions of relational witnessing, holistic integration, and culturally specific wisdom.

A CONTEMPLACOSTAL APPROACH

Any book that includes my story would naturally bring in not only my cultural identities and family background but also my religious background. I was raised in primarily Evangelical and Pentecostal churches, introduced to what Christians call the baptism of the Holy

Introduction

Spirit through the prayers of my father's mother, my grandmother, Irene Yong. When I went on to tertiary education, I did so within these two streams while working as a full-time congregational minister.

Then my spiritual journey took a major turn. I left these spaces to complete my doctoral studies in a more ecumenical and interreligious environment in Southern California. And it was during my time of study there that I was introduced to the contemplative streams within Christianity (and across religious traditions). I found a deep resonance with the experiences and insights I encountered in the contemplatives from across traditions. At that time, I was also introduced to the Christian Church (Disciples of Christ—DOC or Disciples) movement and found within it a vast diversity of congregations open to contemplative spirituality and social justice, as well as an array of ministers who also identified as Pentecostal. Because the movement seemed to hold space for many different elements so important to my spiritual journey, I chose to become ordained as a minister with the DOC and now self-identify as a Pentecostal[3] minister within the Disciples tradition, where I seek to bring my own spiritual legacies to bear on social healing and transformation.

I refer to my personal spirituality as *contempla-costal*—weaving together the empowerment and direct experience of the divine with a relational attitude of holistic liberation that is present in many different

Trauma and Renewal

cultural and spiritual traditions. I view our lived spiritualities as continuously transforming, even as they aim toward living in greater connection with the Whole. It is also with the backdrop of contemplacostal spirituality that I turn to primary themes from the Pentecost narrative within Acts 1 and 2 in structuring this book. The three themes that inform the three primary sections of this book are those of *witness*, *visions*, and *liberative community* (where the many tongues[4] and languages of the world are evidenced, affirmed, and embraced). What I appreciate about these themes are the ways in which they are truly Christian and open the door to enrichment through relationship with diverse traditions.

Guided by my contemplacostal approach, I turn to intercultural exploration with a conviction that no one perspective can adequately reveal or speak to the fullness of our experiences. Performatively, then, the many tongues of Pentecost invite an intercultural approach to trauma transformation by embracing diverse spiritual, secular, and psychological insights grounded in the practice of testimony,[5] which births personal and relational capacities of weaving suffering and joy together.

One way of speaking about my spiritual approach to trauma transformation is as a long loving look at the multiple facets of personal suffering which connects us to the experience of the Whole. This, of course, does not mean all suffering is the same, but rather is intended to create within us opportunities for curiosity, empathy,

Introduction

and cultivating deeper compassion toward ourselves and others. We are not meant to suffer alone. From an intercultural perspective, a focus on connecting to the Whole is in harmony with multiracial, Indigenous, and Asian American sensibilities whose identities have been forged through systemic oppression and while maintaining hopes of collective flourishing. Interestingly, while there have been a growing number of theologians who have connected cultural values[6] to Christian contextual theologies, there have been few accounts that take into consideration the presence and experience of trauma and none inviting intergenerational, intercultural, and psychospiritual processes of transformation. In this light, I find it of great value to wed together one's spirituality, skills around trauma care, and cultural wisdom so that the holistic experiences each of us brings can be remembered and tended.

For so many who identify as spiritual or religious today, there is a misconception about the purpose of spirituality, where most primarily focus on individual well-being. While personal well-being is important, a genuine spirituality from contemplative perspectives goes far beyond individual happiness and must include creating spaciousness within oneself for attending to the suffering of the whole world. For me, the teachings of Christian mystics are helpful, especially those who have written their own memoirs. Contemplatives, such as St. John of the Cross, Julian of Norwich, Howard Thurman, and Thomas Merton, have each documented their confrontation with various dimensions

Trauma and Renewal

of personal and societal suffering along with possibilities of transformation. My intention is to continue this tradition and articulate how contemporary trauma transformation is enhanced through application of the ancient wisdom of Christian mysticism and contemplation brought together with the insights and spiritualities from diverse cultural traditions. As I see it, spirituality is most helpful when it comes to trauma transformation as a way of finding enough capacity to return to the suffering with compassion and connection rather than avoidance or a saviorism. I am not proposing a contemplacostal spirituality as a one size fits all for each person, but rather share it as one path of creative integration and expression that calls us to deeper love for our embodied experiences and all of life.

When it comes to my spiritual story, there have been elements I've necessarily parted ways with (especially explicit and subtle forms of religious superiority or ethnocentrism), and so my own holistic healing has involved reclaiming liberative wisdoms from within my own cultural heritage that have been historically demonized or dismissed. Perhaps you too have an idiosyncratic spiritual heritage and struggle to claim the minoritized aspects of your story. My invitation to you is to identify what threads in your own spiritual journey are meaningful, what it looks like to embrace them, and to confront what has been harmful, and transform your approach to the tradition so that your spiritual story is life affirming for you and others.

Introduction

AN OUTLINE

As I wrote earlier, the book is structured in three main sections: *witness, visions,* and *liberative community,* each carrying significant intercultural implications for tending to trauma relationally. In Part I, I focus on bearing witness to trauma in all its multidimensional suffering. In Part II, I relate how trauma transformation may be catalyzed through dreams, visions, and other alternative states of consciousness calling us to engage suffering with sacred wisdom. And in Part III, I entertain the possibilities of interrelationship in co-creating liberative, intercultural, and trauma transforming communities.

All three chapters in Part I circle around the ineffability of trauma, the harrowing long-term effects of trauma, and the multiple relational dimensions of impact. I relate firsthand experience of being hit by an automobile and of being left vulnerable in the middle of a freeway. My father, Amos, and my mother, Alma, experienced secondary trauma: my mother as she was on a call with me when it happened, and my father, as he later received the phone call that nobody ever wants to receive about their child. In this part the primary focus is on recounting the pain and suffering that was unbearable.

Part II focuses on the series of visions I experienced during my thirty-day hospital stay in 2018. Here, I explore the sacred dimensions hidden and interwoven

Trauma and Renewal

with suffering as I reckon with life in all its polarities and contradictions. I discuss the radicality of my experience and how that transformed the way I view life. In this part, I invite you to imagine how the sacred is calling you to a different engagement with trauma and I also affirm the call for each of us (and every part of us) to be received fully and wholly in love.

The final part is devoted to sharing the importance of co-creating liberative and intercultural communities that are trauma informed and trauma transforming. The chapters in this section emphasize the unending invitations to continuous trauma transformation through the cultivation of daily, embodied practices. The invitations are not to live predetermined or mechanistic lives, overplanned and overstructured (a tool from colonization), but to live each day in its creative dynamism, open and ready to engage what may come.

In each part I detail portions of my own lived experiences of surviving trauma, along with glimpses into my parents' experiences as secondary trauma survivors, as well as contemplative reflections on the nature of trauma and transformation, psychological and cultural inquiry, and the integration of personal and relational practices for trauma. Paradigms of wholeness that deny the mysterious aspects of suffering are ones I resist throughout the book. It feels vital that we regain our sense of the sacred nature of healing so that it can empower us as we face immense challenges of doubt, shame, self-loathing,

Introduction

and despair on the trauma-transformation path. It turns out that trauma transformation *must be* holistic and a lifelong engagement if it is to be fruitful. The healing process is neither linear nor easily understood rationally but can be deepened through intentional community. In this last part, we'll explore how emergent models of relational healing help us to reimagine Christian spirituality for today so that it can be more psychologically, interculturally, and collectively informed.

Finally, in the Afterword, I provide a short self-reflection on the process of writing and healing that I and my community of caregivers traversed, and I reflect on how our lived experiences of ongoing dis/ability, multiraciality, Latin Americanness, and Asian Americanness, shaped the process.

This book reflects an ongoing process of trauma transformation that I hope you, as you read, feel invited to engage as we cocreate and corealize wholeness together.

PART I

WITNESS

1

UNKNOWING

It started as a day of profound joy. I felt the wind on my face and the sun on my back as I rode my motorcycle home, excited to see my spouse and our two young children (our second child was born just a few months earlier). I headed home from a grueling multiday defense of my oral exams at the midway point in my PhD program. The road was familiar, a thirty-mile trek I enjoyed as I was filled with relief after passing the exams.

I looked forward to being home, enthusiastic to celebrate the milestone, and then ready myself to fully focus on writing my dissertation. The day was meant to be one of jubilation—and there is no way I could have envisioned the life-changing events about to unfold.

In the blink of an eye, I was blindsided by a Ford F-150 pickup truck, gargantuan in comparison to the size of the small cruiser I rode. With a vicious blow, I was thrown off my bike, my body hurled hundreds of feet, my right leg skidding into pavement, taking the brunt of the injury. While I hadn't worn protective pants or shoes, thankfully, I had on a protective jacket and helmet.

Trauma and Renewal

Skidding on the front of my leg created a road burn with a gaping opening of ripped-out bone, flesh, and tendon. From my knee to my ankle the open wound now filled with black asphalt.

On this day, October 16, 2018, everything I understood about my life radically changed. Trauma has a way of changing everything—that is if you survive a traumatic event. Whether the trauma is connected to a specific one-time event or a series of chronically repeated events or trauma caused by the systemic factors of oppression, war, ecological disaster, or intergenerational forces, the bottom line is this: Trauma leaves lasting marks on our lives and the spiritual scars remain with us for as long as we live.[1]

Trauma, with its long-term effects, according to the American Psychological Association (APA), is "an emotional response to a terrible event like an accident, rape, or natural disaster." The APA explains that "immediately after the event, shock and denial are typical. Longer-term reactions include unpredictable emotions, flashbacks, strained relationships, and even physical symptoms like headaches or nausea."[2] We'll look at how trauma affects not just our emotional life and mental state, but our physical body, our spiritual person, especially when moral injury occurs, and the many intimate relations that support us as we move together in this book.

Unknowing

While there are many different types of trauma, and they are all important to understand, it is essential to recognize that what they all have in common is that trauma is involuntary and inescapable. In other words, it is the kind of suffering we go through that we don't desire and that we wish to avoid. Trauma involves those experiences that leave our lives hanging in the balance, and because of this intensity, it has lasting impacts on our whole person and upsets our capacities to make sense of what happened.

We also know that trauma affects not only the individual living through its impact but also those affected secondhand, either because the individual witnessed a traumatic event or has heard about a story of trauma from another. Secondary trauma can also occur when supporting another as a primary trauma companion. In short, trauma is not just about individuals but about the damage done to our most cherished relationships, whether it be the divine, those close to us, the more-than-human world, or our relationship to ourselves. While there is a lot we do not understand about trauma, one thing seems certain: The deeper we go into the human experience, the more likely we will confront trauma within and/or through our interconnectedness to others.

Though trauma is multifaceted and multidimensional, with significant divergences case by case, most agree that trauma affects us all—and it seems to be escalating. No

Trauma and Renewal

person can live in this world without experiencing or witnessing a trauma, whether great or small, and in an era of environmental degradation we are witnessing the trauma of mother earth herself.[3] It is not a matter of if but when. For some, trauma starts before or during the birth process: This is evident in cases where mothers experience posttraumatic stress disorder during the pregnancy, and this carries over to impact the fetus.[4] Just under 50 percent of mothers report birth trauma, which results in nearly one out of five infants sustaining physical and psychological injuries during birth.

Although trauma meets some of us in our earliest moments and infiltrates life universally, the manifestations and nuances of trauma are extremely intimate and personal. No two trauma (or posttraumatic growth) stories are alike. Look at the example of twins who survive birth trauma and are born minutes apart. While many aspects of their experience are in common, there are examples where long-term effects on each one can be substantially different. Posttraumatic sufferings range from feelings of hopelessness, despair, isolation, and a sense of instability, and the ways they are felt varies widely and greatly from person to person and situation to situation. Therefore, it is important to know that when it comes to trauma care, there is no one-size-fits-all approach. We all must find our own unique ways of tending trauma and are invited to make space for others as they find theirs.

Unknowing

If the near-death motorcycle accident I lived through did not seem "bad" on its own, it gets even more gut wrenching. The moment before it happened, I was on a call via my Bluetooth headset with my mother, Alma, whom I had called to share how my exams went, and she shared how proud she was of me as I reached this milestone in my academic journey. What began as a call of celebration and affirmation turned quickly into one of grave emergency. All I could utter after the fall was, "Mom, I have been hit. I am lying in the middle of the freeway!" She immediately called 911.

As she hung up the phone, I felt the gravity of being all alone. While I was in shock to the physical pain, I wondered to myself, *Is this how it all ends? I wish I could tell my family how much I love them. What about my children? How will they grow up without their father?*

As I lay there, I was aware neither of the severity of my injury nor of the threat of being run over by oncoming traffic; but I *was* aware of the possibility of my life coming to an end. I began to pray. As I reflect on the incident, it was not that I *chose* to pray or prayed as some act of will. Rather, it was as if a prayer arose from somewhere within me, from some place I do not fully understand. The prayer that arose was a prayer of complete desperation.

During most of the previous decade leading to this time, I had been a Pentecostal minister working in a congregational setting. I had spent many hours praying (publicly and privately) and was well versed in the performance of public prayer. In addition, I was raised in a ministerial family, where my grandparents on both sides were Pentecostal converts as adults whose own radical experiences of healing and conversion to Pentecostal Christianity led them to become ordained and lay ministers, whom I would often see praying in public and at home. In this lineage, I knew prayer. At least, I thought I did.

Yet in the moment of my greatest need, the prayer that came forth was of an entirely different nature. Words were not recognizable. I stammered, pleading for help. The prayer became filled with the practice I had known in other moments of my life, moments more joyous and life affirming, what is known as praying in the Spirit. Though I had prayed in the Spirit before, it was never like that. All I remember from that time between when my mother hung up to call for help and the time an ambulance came is that my prayer intensified with every moment that passed by as I became more and more conscious of the pain.

ALMA'S REFLECTION

Almost every weekday afternoon my son and I would have our daily phone calls about our day. I always looked forward—and still do—to our chats about what is happening. And this day (October 16, 2018) was very special, since it was

Unknowing

the last day of his qualifying oral exams, a major milestone in his doctoral program.

I was eager to congratulate him on his passing his exams with distinction. I have always been very proud of my son, and I have said many times, "I do not know what I did to be your mom! I am a blessed woman."

Initially, he and I were planning to begin doctoral programs together, but I had to defer, so seeing him come to this point was exciting and a very happy occasion. As we were rejoicing together, I suddenly heard him say, "Mom, I was just hit!" He said it first in a normal calm voice and I could not believe I had heard him correctly; yet, within a second, I could hear the sound of him in deep pain. This was a pain that pierced my innermost being, and all I could think was "Help!"

So, I hung up, pulled over, called 911, and let the 911 respondent know where my son was located. To this day, I do not know how I hung up the phone and called 911. Our call was my lifeline to him. And ending the phone call with him, not knowing if that was the last time I would talk to him, was one of the most difficult decisions I have ever made: to hang up on my hurting son.

I then began to pray to God for protection and cried out loud that he would be okay, that angels would protect him, that he would sense God's presence all around him, that he would not feel alone. I prayed that people would come around him and protect and help him, that he would be safe on that busy Southern California highway.

I had to calm myself down from crying, and I finally called my husband, Amos, telling him what happened. He asked to stay where I was, and not to drive, knowing I was too distraught to drive safely.

As I write this reflection, my heart and spirit well up with the immensity of that moment. Amid my tears, I continue to be grateful that God answered every prayer in that moment. That remains an almost unimaginable moment, when a mother hears her son in so much pain. Recalling it now, still is heart wrenching. Yet it is God alone who sustains and delivers us.

AMOS'S REFLECTION

As I begin to recall those moments after the accident, I sense the many questions, many feelings—including great desperation and anxiousness—which beset me. However, the response that was the strongest within me was the sense I needed to be patient, to be steady, as everything else was out of our hands.

Everything remains a blur. I have dim recollections about initially seeing my son in the hospital, sensing his pain and feeling quite helpless to address or ease his agony. I do not remember too much; perhaps this was "normal" due to the shock of it all. I just was glad Aizaiah was still with us.

Being the eldest male in a Chinese–Malaysian immigrant family who moved to the United States when I was just a boy, "being steady," was the only coping mechanism I felt any access to. What has transpired over the last half decade plus since the accident has encouraged me to continue pressing into the some of the more fundamental questions of who I am, especially as an Asian/Chinese American immigrant, and why I responded as I did, rather than in other, perhaps more emotionally felt ways. Now, in wishing to explore my own limitations to trauma response, at least at the emotional level, I want to locate these constraints, name them, as they were squarely in the realm of my being inadequately in touch with my embodied self as a Chinese American 1.5 generation (that is, born in Malaysia but raised in the United States) immigrant.[5]

Many with my background would start here, with the Chinese or Confucian side of this equation. While my Christian parents (Pentecostal pastors since before I, their eldest son, was born) did not make much explicitly of Confucian ways of being in the world, they still held, perhaps unintentionally, Confucian ways. As first-generation converts inculcated by the ministry of American Pentecostal missionaries, they were told of the importance of leaving their Chinese cultural ways behind—my father's Malaysian-bred Hakka-ness and my mother's Hokkien-ness meant we were raised according to East Asian understandings of filial piety, even as these doctrines were rarely mentioned or elaborated on. Within the Confucian family, fathers are feared, distant, stern, and remote disciplinarians, and sons, especially the firstborn like I was, related more emotionally and affectionately with their mothers.[6] As I look back on my own upbringing, that is how I experienced both of my parents growing up. Once, when my father was very late picking me up from my elementary school, I remember running to my mother and crying hard in her embrace.[7] But when my father disciplined me, I learned how to withhold my tears, to be tough, to learn from my mistakes and never repeat them, if possible.

Now that I reflect on these last five years and my own response to Aizaiah's trauma, of the accident and the aftermath, I note both my inability to remember or to feel much. I believe this is indicative of my having overcompensated throughout my life with my cognitive abilities. In these various respects, as a 1.5 generation Chinese American, my Western upbringing and education have thoroughly assimilated me into Euro-American values, not least the "I think, therefore I am" standard of the modernist individual.

Now, according to all conventional expectations, I have fulfilled my filial role as father to Aizaiah: "The father must provide for his sons when they are young, educate them in the ancestral tradition, find mates for them, and leave them good names and inheritances as well as he can,"[8] is one way in which these fatherly obligations are delineated. And I had done what needed to be done.

And yet, because of my history being primed intellectually and cognitively, the embodied and emotional side of who I was, and who we as father and son could be, was unreachable. While mentally, I was able to perceive my son's accident, beyond that, I was unable to connect with myself or him.

Unknowing

As the aftermath of trauma haunts and perplexes survivors and caregivers alike, growing consensus points to tending to trauma in ways that require holistic approaches that engage the body, mind, and spirit of each person, and ideally will involve the whole network of those connected to the person traumatized.

Earlier I mentioned how differently people respond to trauma. There are many factors that play into this: one's lived experiences; social location; family history; and according to an increasing number of neuroscientists and psychologists, one's spirituality. While many religious communities certainly cause and perpetuate their own forms of trauma, religious communities and spiritual teachings also hold potential to recover and heal.[9] More specifically, there is a case to be made for the ways spirituality (which involves, the various paths or practices that help support deeper experiences of connection and relationship to the whole) is complementary to but distinct from religion's institutional and intellectual dimensions,[10] and therefore spirituality can even be encouraged when tending to trauma, especially when the person or community who is traumatized is familiar with spirituality being a source of refuge through difficult life circumstances.[11]

We can see the power of embracing spirituality in tending to trauma holistically when we look to the African spirituals and the songs sung in unity such as "We Shall Overcome!" or in the story of Indra's Net

Trauma and Renewal

in Buddhism or in the Melting the Ice in the Heart of Man teaching from the Kalaallit Nunaat Peoples. Through these examples, we find the power of spiritually empowered trauma transformation and how this has long been true in more communal cultures throughout the global majority.[12]

If we allow some of these marginalized cultures (due to forces of empire and colonization) to guide us, we begin to see how healing is not just about an individual but that which moves us toward honoring communion with all of life. Take, for example, the *Taki Oncoy* resistance movement led by Indigenous Peoples who opposed Spanish colonization in the region now known as the Peruvian Andes. The power of their resistance was in the ways they would dance and sing to be in rhythm and sacred connection with the "Great community, Network of Life, Pachamama," including their own ancestors who had been murdered by the colonizers.[13] For the Aymara Peoples, the way to pursue harmony and liberation was to be in embodied harmonious relationship with one another and the land, refusing to accept a status of subjugation promoted by their oppressors.

In Confucian cultures, there is a profound understanding that trauma is an experience that has potential to lead us toward a deeper realization of our own shared humanity characterized by contingency and an opportunity for ever-deepening meaning and purpose. Confucian philosopher Tu Wei-ming comments that it

Unknowing

is "through pain and suffering, we form one body with our fellow human beings, with other animals, with trees and plants, and with stones and tiles."[14] For Wei-ming, this oneness is not a homogenous reality but a sense of knowing our interdependence with others. A Confucian sensibility would also advocate for the minimization of harm as much as is possible, even recognizing that existence itself is inherently filled with danger, threat, and risk. And while there is a place to differentiate between pain, sorrow, suffering,[15] and trauma, for our purposes it's important to note that each of these is part and parcel of the human experience, therefore we should do our best to do no harm to one another and to avoid adding to the suffering that is already there.

In the Confucian tradition, even the greatest of suffering can become an experience that awakens us to a greater fullness of life and power of compassion. In this sense, while trauma has unique repercussions for each being and should be respected and cared for with great sensitivity, trauma also may open us toward a life of solidarity with other beings who suffer. Inspired by the Confucian admission of suffering, we can begin to see how our trauma can be significantly transformed if we are open to the full range of experience being shared together in community.

A third example can be found within the African American tradition. Theologian Barbara Holmes describes the Middle Passage as a collective trauma giving rise to

Trauma and Renewal

"crisis contemplation." Holmes describes the trauma taking place among the enslaved, where out of the unthinkable and involuntary, a "rebirthing" emerged. She writes, "As it turns out, contemplation that arises from a crisis or collective trauma is a displacement of everyday life and a freefall into 'what comes next.' … When the crisis occurs, the only way out is through, so we take a cue from nature and relax into the stillness, depending upon one another and the breath of life!"[16]

For Holmes, trauma cannot adequately be addressed through individualized interventions but requires a "wounded village" to come together, bearing witness to great sorrows carried, and entrusting oneself and the community to the divine. There is a sense with Holmes's contemplative vision that trauma is not just a story for one person to tell but beckons us to share with one another, finding healing through connection rather than isolation or separation.

Again, if we follow the lead of communities of color, we find that trauma transformation can be pursued in more thoroughly relational ways. And we can strengthen our capacities for wholeness when we are open to the sacred force that binds us together (whether we use the same language or symbol for that force). In practice, this means that whether they be first responders, family members, or friends—trauma transformation involves the engagement of many around us and is sustained best when supported by a loving community or network of care.

Unknowing

While I cannot describe the trauma I endured as "spiritual" (in fact what I lived through seems beyond a description of words), what I do know is that my lived spirituality was eternally transformed that day and the ones that followed.

Prior to my accident, I would have considered myself a devoutly spiritual person. I was always drawn to the experiential, personal, and empowering dimension of religious life. And for me, the most deeply spiritual moments often emerged outside of the institutional church, making me question why religious institutions seemed to be so devoid of living spirituality. It was, oddly enough, my deep yearning for a wholesome and inclusive spirituality that drew me to pursue graduate studies. Yet in the immediate moments of consciousness after I was hit, I felt utterly unprepared with what I knew of spirituality up to that point. Much of what I had been taught spiritually provided little support during the present catastrophe. I was hurled into a place beyond anything I had known.

If you have lived through trauma or secondary trauma yourself, you, too, may experience the abyss like a groundless territory of the suffering. In the abyss, there seem to be few options. None that are promising. We are left undone, and it is there we must rebuild our lived spiritualities from the fragments.

Perhaps it is precisely the presence of radical unknowing, which engenders experiences of trauma, that also creates a portal to the sacred. When it comes to trauma in any

Trauma and Renewal

circumstance or context, there is nothing that should be idealized or romanticized. And somehow, we also note how spiritualities emerged precisely from trauma, foremost among those accounts in the Hebrew and Christian scriptures.[17] Personal and collective trauma was the foundation in Israel's many struggles and hopes for liberation. And trauma indeed was a major dynamic undergirding the day of Pentecost (viewed as the birth of the Christian church) as the early followers of Jesus found themselves paralyzed by fear, waiting in the upper room after their Messiah and spiritual leader, Jesus of Nazareth, was murdered, as they held (albeit weakly) a promise of what was to come—the gift of the Holy Spirit.[18] But their questions outnumbered their hope in the promise. How would this work? How would they know? How long would it take? I wonder if the disciples felt quite alone.

The disciples who gathered that day in the upper room had many reasons to fear. Yes, the resurrected Jesus appeared for forty days, but had left them again. Still, they had more questions than answers. What was the baptism of the Spirit that Jesus spoke of? And what difference would it make during such significant grief, loss, and oppression? How would they cope while so many of those they loved were also grieving and being persecuted for their faith? In their widespread uncertainty, they were instructed to wait, as the Book of Acts records, to wait on the promise of Jesus's spirit.

I imagine the prayers they were offering came from fear, and held pleas for help, too. Perhaps that, mixed

Unknowing

in with confusion, anxiety, restlessness, flashbacks of the trauma they had just witnessed. While Jesus promised they would never be alone, he was crucified and separated from them. It certainly felt like they were alone now, unsure of what would come next; yet it was precisely this uncertainty in them that would create an opening to relearn and rebuild their own lives, and to do so together in community.

"The surprising thing is that the intimate healing that spirituality brings into our lives is often hidden in the muck and mire of the very things about ourselves we wish were not true,"[19] writes James Finley, a survivor of childhood abuse. As a spiritual director and psychotherapist, Finley has devoted his vocation to tending trauma through spirituality. He has traveled throughout the world teaching about the promises and perils of trauma work and highlights the profound resources that spirituality can offer. What Finley refers to as *hiddenness*, is exactly the kind of radical unknowing that trauma survivors must face. This hiddenness is why trauma is often so mired, leaving those who survive it feeling lost and alone. And for this reason, it is all so important we journey through trauma transformation in community. Although we experience the inescapable, involuntary, and life-altering nature of trauma, our lived spiritualities practiced in community can serve as a bridge toward possibilities of becoming something wholly, completely, and altogether new.

Trauma and Renewal

PERSONAL PRACTICE OF GENTLE UNKNOWING

1. Bring to this practice a piece of paper and a colored pencil or crayon.
2. Attempt to draw something with your nondominant hand that is comforting to you. It could be a place you enjoy, a symbol that is important to you, or people whom you love.
3. It is okay to lean into any discomfort from the practice, moving slowly with yourself.
4. Stay curious about what's forming inside yourself as you draw. If any harsh judgments arise, you might ask yourself why that's coming up.
5. After you finish, take a moment to reflect on any thoughts, beliefs, or feelings the practice brings up.
6. It is common for us to feel disoriented and vulnerable when asked to do something we are not as familiar with. We may feel challenged, exposed, or lost. If any of these aspects were present within you, inform those parts within that experienced a sense of unknowing or disorientation that they are loved.

RELATIONAL PRACTICE OF EXTENDING CIRCLES OF COMPASSION

1. Bring to mind someone you deeply love. Using your breath as an anchor, extend love and care toward them. So, for example, during an in-breath, you might send them loving connection. And during the out-breath you might send them abiding peace. Take about two minutes to do this.

Unknowing

2. Repeat this process again, now with a friend in mind.
3. Do this once more, now bringing a stranger to mind.
4. Notice what you experience for each circle of compassion and what arises in you. Be curious about any resistance you may sense.
5. Honor where you are in the process and move at a pace that feels right to you.

2

WITH-NESS-ING

In many Eurocentric cultures, individualism and rationalism are privileged, and this might be why trauma is of such great interest to modern science and why it has turned into a ubiquitous phenomenon. Trauma unravels any sense of individual autonomy, agency, or independence, and those who endure it are left without much sense of self or explanation about what happened. Perhaps, there is no other clearer representation of a Eurocentric approach to trauma as Bessel van der Kolk's *The Body Keeps the Score: Brain, Mind, and Body in the Healing of Trauma*, which has become a *locus classicus* in understanding the varied and embodied dimensions of human traumatization.[1] Van der Kolk's starting point is the neuroscience and neurobiology of trauma, and he details how trauma activates our body's alarm or stress reactivity mechanisms that move us into flight or fight modes. Study after study reveals that when experiencing traumatic flashbacks, the limbic or behavioral and emotional portion of the brain that sits on the right side above the oldest brain layer—the so-called reptilian

With-ness-ing

brain—lights up, while the neocortex at the top of our brain (responsible for our speech and rationality) is subdued. Thus, upon recognizing a troubling situation, our central nervous system prompts us to escape (flight), or, if necessary, galvanizes us to ward off the intruding hostility (fight); when neither is possible, we find ourselves trapped, in which case our bodies' self-preservation efforts involve "shutting down and expending as little energy as possible. We are then in a state of *freeze* or *collapse*."[2] In my journey through trauma, I have faced all three.

But as I've previously noted, there is more to trauma than the individual impacts. If we consider a more relational standpoint aligned with Indigenous and East Asian cosmologies, we see that trauma creates a distortion of our perception of time and space and presents a window into life being re-created. When everything came undone for me at a personal level, there was a sense in which everything painfully slowed down but also a paradoxical feeling that life was coming at me with full speed and full force. The distortion of time and space is agonizing, and in many moments, I was not sure I could go any further. Trauma signals to us that the life we once knew is forever lost, and the life we are now experiencing is beyond comprehension. It may be the multifaceted ways that trauma disrupts our capacities to make sense of things that links nonlinearity[3] and liminality[4] to trauma transformation. Trauma launches us into

Trauma and Renewal

an experience of liminality because we begin to sense that our personhood is more of an ongoing lived journey rather than a static one. Trauma is an intense in-breakage into the personal stories we once believed were coherent and comprehensible, and we find our experience is much more susceptible and vulnerable to the actions of others.

As I lay there in the middle of the freeway, I remember asking myself the haunting question, *Is this what it feels like to die?* And soon after asking myself that question, I began to feel the onset of the excruciating pain that would accompany me in the days and months ahead. I then thought, *I must not be dying because the amount of pain I am feeling makes me feel alive in the worst way!*

In the days that followed, I would often feel a sharp sensation as though my body were being ripped open violently. The entire right side of my body was a road rash, as large pieces of flesh on my arm, side, and waist had been ripped open. Most of the damage, however, was to the front part of my lower leg, between my knee and ankle. The entire front half of my right leg was gone, and I felt the sensation as though my leg was set on fire without any ability to put it out.

The police officer who was the first professional help to approach me that day asked me about my pain level. I replied, *words are not adequate to describe the pain!* He told me to hang in there and that more help was on the way. I remember asking him directly, *Do you think I am*

With-ness-ing

going to die? He could not look me in the eye, replying with any comforting answer. The only thing he could say was, "Just hang in there."

I asked him to promise me that if I did not live that he would tell my partner and children that I was thinking of them in these moments and that my love for them was eternal. While the police report of the accident states that the firefighters came about twenty minutes after the police, I assure you the waiting felt like hours on end.

When the firefighters finally arrived, they quickly transferred me to their firetruck, and I was transported to the local hospital. With the indescribable pain I was in, I felt it exacerbated with every bump and sharp turn in the road. I recall asking the firefighters if they had anything they could do to alleviate the pain and they, too, responded by telling me to "hold on" and the hospital would take care of me.

When the pain was so great that it seemed too much to bear, I turned to the stoic firefighter there next to me and asked if he would hold my hand. His look was one of disapproval and awkwardness. I thought to myself, *How did I find myself at such a low point? And how will I endure?* But I reached for his hand anyway and refused to let it go until we arrived at the hospital.

The emergency room is not the place anyone wants to die. It is filled with desperation and the sounds of the shrieks and moans of those with life-threatening injuries.

Trauma and Renewal

The twelve hours I spent there felt like a lifetime. To my left, was a person who was suffering from severe mental distress and all alone. To my right, was a family arguing about end-of-life plans surrounding their family member who was on the verge of transitioning. I could hear their frustrations, blame, and anxieties building.

In the middle of both these worlds, I waited for my loved ones to arrive. On top of the physical pain, I felt an ocean of shame. Even though I was not at fault, I felt ashamed that I had been hit, fearing how this would forever change me as a parent and the impacts it would have on my kids. I felt responsible for perhaps never becoming the father I thought I was supposed to be, the father I needed to be to protect my children from the violence of the world.

I questioned why I had ever said yes to riding a motorcycle in the first place when so many others had told me that it was not a matter of "if, but when" a life-threatening accident would transpire. *I should have known better,* I thought, *but now my choice may have cost me and those I love the ultimate price.* The self-critical voices welled up inside me. However, the physical pain was so strong and soon overwhelmed the self-pitying narratives. I was desperate for relief in any form I could get it. But I was too weak to move my body on my own and with every passing moment my strength decreased.

As my partner and parents arrived at the emergency room, I felt another wave of regret come over me. I

With-ness-ing

hoped that no person would ever see me in a condition of complete brokenness—especially those I loved so dearly. I could not muster up many words, but tears began to flow from my eyes. And I felt some comfort knowing I was no longer all alone. I thanked them for coming and told them I loved them with all my being.

How is a person who is "frozen" or "collapsed" to manage in an individualistic society where the dominant values are autonomy and agency? The answer is, not well at all. Some might find it more desirable to die than be rendered impotent, damaged, and flawed due to trauma. For it is one thing to die and for one's life to be over, but it is a different kind of torment to remain alive and feel totally helpless and dependent on others. This is the logic of an individualistic society.

And the struggles to transform trauma are only exacerbated for all those bodies marginalized by race, class, gender, sexuality, or ability—among other identities—for the stakes of disclosing trauma are tied to the fear that any vulnerability that is exposed will be exploited. Compare this to my experience as an adult, where my initial reaction toward my suffering was self-shaming and internalized hatred for vulnerability.

We know that trauma does not simply heal with time but persists and wreaks invisible havoc hidden in the depths of our consciousness; when untended, the horrors remain somewhere deep under our skin, and we feel it in

Trauma and Renewal

our bones. And not only does the pain remain within us but when unresolved, begins to touch and unravel those who are in close relationship with us. In short, trauma leaves us disillusioned with the cultural and societal myths that prioritize individualistic ideas. Many new paradigms are warranted.

One of the important insights from trauma care studies shows the importance of tending to trauma through the relational act of witnessing,[5] a way of embodied presence that is deeply undergirded and guided by the power of compassion. Some call this act of being present *witnessing,* which is a subtle act and differs greatly from a posture of fixing the problem. While witnessing can involve responsive action for a person suffering, the focus of the witness is on being with another in the fullness of their experience and demonstrating unconditional positive regard for the person in trauma and their experience.

This posture is what I call "with-ness-ing." There are many reasons why with-ness-ing, or being compassionately present to the suffering of another (without being paralyzed or overwhelmed by it), is of far more value than simply striving for a solution, as, say, the professional, the medical practitioner, or the therapist might aim to do. The first reason is practical and lies in the fact that healing has no timetable and there is no one-size-fits-all approach. Every person's path to recovery is unique, and the process toward integration is non-linear.

With-ness-ing

To impose how, when, or what healing should look like, therefore, only results in dehumanizing a person's experience and increases the suffering one is in because it adds to the person's sense of something being wrong with them.

The second reason that with-ness-ing is vital when it comes to tending trauma is because of the deep isolation and abandonment that accompanies the traumatized person. What was lost in trauma is precisely what is needed for healing to occur, namely, the experience of relationship, positive regard, and caring affirmation.

Finally, while traumatized persons are never able to fully or adequately express the suffering they have endured, having other beings (sacred, cosmic, or human) show up for them with a deep sense of respect and honor for that person's experience yields restorative qualities, opens possibilities for reframing and renarrating what has happened in ways beyond words. This presence and respect carry unforeseen potential.

Within the Christian contemplative tradition there are diverse examples of with-ness-ing found in those who have traversed great depths of suffering themselves, not least the Christ who experienced the passion. Those closest to Christ were forced to ask the very difficult, harrowing, and poignant question, Is there any comfort in the middle of chaos?

Perhaps we find a sense of Christ's with-ness-ing amid our inability to answer this question when we look

Trauma and Renewal

to the story of Jesus's mother who was distraught in losing her son, or to the example of the many disciples who after Christ's crucifixion, were unable to recognize the resurrected Christ due to the trauma they recently experienced. For it is their sense of destabilization that affirms to us our own experiences of the abyss-like nature of trauma.

Or in a more positive light, we might consider the apophatic-oriented contemplative Christians who teach us to make a place within ourselves for all that we do not understand. The Spanish mystic St. John of the Cross is among those who wrote extensively about this process, what he referred to as the dark night of the soul. One of his most famous quotes, reads, "Oh night, more lovely than the dawn."[6] And it is precisely his journey and descent into hell, that makes his account trustworthy to us in guiding us amid our feelings of loss, lost-ness, and without much idea of what will come next. The with-ness-ing that we experience from people like John of the Cross involves accepting reality as the "night" it is and then responding to it with love and creative connection.

The practice of with-ness-ing I just described is a radical alternative to many contemporary psychological models that assume individualistic ideals and fixate upon diagnosing and treating symptoms so that people can become more individualized (often requiring a dependence on never-ending prescription drugs). While there is great importance in helping others identify acute

With-ness-ing

symptoms and to find symptom relief through medicine (again this should not be minimized), there is another, more holistic healing that is relational and hinges upon extending radical nonviolence toward one's suffering within the context of the suffering of others. Our suffering—as our wholeness—is all interconnected.

Within contemporary models of trauma transformation, there are a few from across diverse cultural traditions that offer spiritually animated, relational paradigms: Restorative justice,[7] touching the earth,[8] and the SOUL practice[9] are among those I have found helpful and inspiring.

Another model of trauma transformation is Internal Family Systems (IFS), which I've trained in and practiced for the past decade. IFS is a psychospiritual model of trauma care that is radically nonpathologizing, pluralistic, dialogical, emergent, and is built around the foundational presence of the Self. *The Self* in this context is a source of innate and embodied wisdom at the core of each person who is imbued with curiosity, confidence, compassion, clarity, creativity, courage, connectedness, and calm. The aim of IFS is both to affirm the multiplicity of "parts" (or ego states) within each person's experience, and to restore each "part" to connection with the Self. The transformational aspect of the model occurs when each "part" can experience the "Self" and become "Self-led."

Self-led means that various parts within us no longer need to be polarized or separate from one another, where

Trauma and Renewal

each part feels the need to do everything alone. Self-leadership is an affirmation of the rich diversity within each person, where every aspect of our lives is invited into creative and harmonious relationship. And as such, IFS is a person-centered and culturally adaptative model that seeks to reconnect the traumatized aspects of a person to the presence of Self. When this happens, people are freed from the need to "act out" whether it be through extreme judgments, behaviors, addictions, or attitudes.

It is important to note that in IFS the healing never comes alone. The key is to relationally connect to the Self within (or sometimes at first the Self of the practitioner, which is offered in the attempt to support reestablishing connection of the person to the Self within). Because IFS is a relational model, IFS practitioners take very seriously the unique inner landscape of each person, following the parts within a person that are traumatized, allowing these parts to lead the way to wholeness rather than prescribing or preplanning an outcome. Practitioners are asked to trust in this poly-vocal process and to stick with it in a gentle, caring, and spacious way. According to IFS perspective, even the most subtle connection to Self is fundamental to the healing path and should not be minimized or overlooked.

The places we begin the path of deep healing in IFS are post-traumatic symptoms, referred to as "trailheads." At first, many learning IFS tend to believe the part that

56

With-ness-ing

holds the burden is the problem; yet IFS teaches that no part of us is the problem, but rather an invitation to learn how to better relate inside. That *better way* of relating in IFS could be an example of what I am describing as with-ness-ing. When our parts inside experience the presence of the Self—a wise and spacious core of connection present in each person—a different way of interaction and integration occurs, which honors the wisdom and life-affirming expression of each part.

IFS offers us both an emergent and relational model for trauma transformation but also shows us the power of embracing the sacred dimensions of healing. Whether it is through the accompaniment of a spiritual director, pastoral leader, therapist, social worker, friend, or another who can hold us in Self-leadership, the presence of tending trauma from a grounded, embodied, and heart-expansive place is paramount.

As we can see, IFS is one concrete example of what "with-ness-ing" can be, since it helps us to see trauma transformation as necessarily including spirituality, relationships of connection, and a way of overcoming individualism without losing the personal. As a spiritual pathway, it involves acceptance of the whole person (including our many diverse parts), finding connection to the Self and parts through compassion and curiosity. It is also spiritual in that it is a model that relies upon a force that is greater than the individual and cannot simply be performed following a training manual or multistep

Trauma and Renewal

process. IFS is intriguing as a spiritually informed trauma practice for diverse communities because it does not require a belief in any particular divine being, but rather relies on a conscious practice of presence, discernment, and dialogue. As a creative practice, the person who is accompanying another must develop a certain comfort with uncertainty and with all that is beyond their understanding. Transformation of trauma is never a naive belief that "all things will work out," where spirituality becomes a form of bypassing and minimization, but rather it is a spirituality of deep attunement and responsiveness and perhaps even open to feeling the suffering of another as the healing arises. It is, more subtly, a giving of oneself to a process that is still unfolding while maintaining a sense of grounded trust in each step.

Although IFS and other models I previously noted cannot be the end and be-all of our trauma transformation practices, they are helpful because they reveal to us the importance of tending to trauma personally, relationally, and holistically in conjunction with our embrace of and seeking strength in our spiritualities. In sum, a practice of with-ness-ing is deeply humanizing, open-ended, and an embodied way of relating to suffering in our communities that moves us beyond certainties and logical explanations. It involves a practice of love bathed in sincerity, curiosity, and a deep connection to wisdom. Ultimately, with-ness-ing is empowered when we are taught by others through their own lived examples of deeply confronting suffering

With-ness-ing

within themselves and accompanied by those who have voluntarily come alongside us to hold the immensity of the suffering together in a spirit of reverence. This is why tending to trauma is not for the faint of heart and must be tended through intimate relationships with others over time and with profound care. Speaking with each other about trauma, not to mention *living through trauma*, is not something we can confront alone, for we belong to one another.

PERSONAL PRACTICE OF INTERNAL WITH-NESS-ING

1. Allow yourself to bring to awareness the memory of a moment of minor[10] discomfort.
2. Notice and identify (if you can) where that discomfort shows up in your body.
   a. Perhaps it shows up as a word, feeling, thought, emotion, or sensation.
   b. Stay with whatever arises for you, rather than thinking too long about the prompts themselves.
3. Extend a gentle welcome to what you notice. Extend, too, a curiosity to listening to the part of you that has become present in the memory of discomfort.
4. What does this part want to share with you?
   a. Ask it what it is afraid of happening if this part does not show up in this way?
   b. Ask what the part hopes for, for you.

Trauma and Renewal

5. Check in with yourself, asking if what the part shares makes sense to you. If so, validate the concerns and hopes expressed compassionately. If not, you might return to the part and ask those questions again, listening for what resonates.
6. Ask the part what age it knows you to be.
7. Consider, does the part needs updating to relate to who you are today? If it does, invite the part to take in the life experiences that have led you to the present moment.
8. Now you might ask that discomforted part if there is anything else you can do to be more attentive to the needs of this part.
9. As you listen to your interior part requesting your attentiveness to specific needs, commit yourself to making that change now. And perhaps in the coming days take some time to notice how that commitment shifts your perspective on the initial situation that brought you discomfort.

3

BEFRIENDING THE TEARS

In the nine days following my accident, I experienced the most intense physical, emotional, and spiritual pain I have ever encountered. Nothing provided relief. Within the first week, five complex multistep operations were required, one almost every other day. The first four were devoted to cleaning out debris and asphalt from deep inside my leg's open wound. And even as I hoped for some relief following each procedure, my pain persisted and even increased.

Due to my intense pain, the doctors administered the maximum dosages of narcotics. Even so, I recall that every movement my body made felt incredibly challenging and uncomfortable, full of stress. Nothing helped alleviate the suffering, and even as I would lie awake, the pain seemed like a never-ending nightmare.

Even the large dosages of the narcotics given to me failed to provided support, as the side effects were numerous. I lost my appetite. And in the few moments I found rest, I would be awakened by the need to vomit, due to debilitating raging headaches. Meanwhile, I was

Trauma and Renewal

hooked up to intravenous therapy to stay hydrated and was restricted from eating solid foods to be ready for each new surgery. Because I lost a great amount of blood, multiple transfusions were required, with my life at risk. During those nine days, I wondered if there would ever be a way through.

Suffering was not something new to my family of origin. Both of my parents were the eldest in their respective families, and they each grew up in working-class households of color expected to work as young children to help their parents make ends meet. Throughout their lives, they encountered racism, xenophobia, classism, ableism, and sexism.

Because my parents were religiously devout, I grew up with a sense of faith, responsibility, and a desire to contribute to the well-being of our family and the wider world. While the severe challenges my parents faced were distinct from my own journey, I can vividly recall moments in my childhood watching my parents work extremely hard to provide for us, and I heard their concerns about our financial affairs.

Soon their determination and attitude around responsibility became my own. Many times, in my youth, I would seek to cheer up my parents when I sensed their discouragement. If I heard a disagreement, I would try to mediate. I internalized burdensome experiences and felt the weight of things resting on my shoulders. There was no time to feel or express emotion

Befriending the Tears

or deal with personal pain because what pushed on me was the necessity of survival.

All these internalized feelings intensified as I grew up with two younger siblings I was expected to look after, responsible for their actions and well-being. Yet even with all the heaviness associated with being the eldest, there were also moments of great delight. I sought to be the big brother who would provide guidance, protection, and leadership to my siblings. And every success they had, big or small, I celebrated.

But as I laid there helpless in the hospital, all the roles I had learned to play as the eldest in my family system were torn down and deconstructed. In my critical condition, I now confronted the reality that I had nothing to contribute to the ones I loved; I was the one in profound need.

I remember well the feelings of failure. I thought of my life partner and my children. *What kind of father am I now?* And then I thought of my two sisters who were now grown and leading families of their own. I could no longer be there to help them, but as the big brother, I was now vulnerable. No insight to offer. No guidance to provide. No encouragement to share. I thank the divine for both of them as they put their lives on pause to visit me in the hospital and tend to me and my family. The roles were reversed, and now I was the one who would learn what it meant to receive care from them.

Parts of me felt like I was experiencing the worst that could happen, not only because I was in extreme

Trauma and Renewal

pain but because I was put in a position of failing those I loved. I was anxious about my family coming to see me in the hospital in such a humiliating state.

And the challenge for me was not just that my family would see me so exposed but all the care providers at the hospital—nurses, doctors, chaplains, and social workers—as well. As a pastor, I was the one used to providing care for others, showing up in their times of need, being a grounded presence, and one to offer hope. But as I lay in the hospital with my life hanging in the balance, I was desperate for others to offer those things to me. The neighbors and strangers I used to imagine I was called to help now were the ones who saw me completely wrecked and dispossessed, and they became angelic presences of compassion. While the specifics of my accident and aftermath are mine to hold in their detail, those of us who experienced enduring trauma may also relate to the fear, loss, anxiety, aloneness, pain, the internalizing of emotional weight, and the sense of losing agency. And as many of us have come to learn, it is not just the individualized experiences that weigh on us but multiple layers of suffering we must confront when we find our lives completely disjointed.

The compounding effects of physical, psychological, intergenerational, and cultural oppression began to take their toll on me. The carefully constructed image of myself as an independent, wise, helpful, pastor now lay shredded and in disarray. And there was no promise of

Befriending the Tears

recovery in sight. For me, it was now the time to learn who I truly was beyond labels and roles. In the nakedness of my own existence, and in my weakness, I began to entrust my life to the care of others. Not because I had a choice but because I was left without a choice.

One of the biggest posttraumatic challenges we face is around trust. This makes sense, because often trauma is the result of our vulnerability being taken advantage of or because we find ourselves in situations where trust has been stolen from us. It is that violation of trust and a sense of betrayal that can create a belief in those harmed that life is altogether inherently untrustworthy. This is where many trauma survivors understandably become even more calloused and desensitized to suffering (their own and that of others) after going through extreme events: It feels like too much to bear, and life has left us without anyone to trust.

Another possible response to trauma is a completely different reaction. Some trauma survivors feel the need to save the world at all costs and seek to become a hero to others. Both responses, however, strip away from us the fullness of our human experience. In the former, we begin to see ourselves as incapable of integrating suffering, so we seek to avoid it as often as we can whether by dismissing it, overlooking it, minimizing or downplaying it. In the latter, we imagine ourselves beyond and above suffering. It causes us to internalize

Trauma and Renewal

suffering as something inherently wrong and therefore in need of saving or fixing, something we believe we must do by our own effort. Regretfully, many spiritualities we are taught (or have inherited) are used to defend both ego-driven responses when they come into or out of us. But there is in fact another way, one that does not reject our suffering or try to make meaning out of it (both options are ultimately dishonest), but rather calls us to walk with and through suffering, offering it back to reality so that it might be transformed to affirm life.

Howard Thurman once said, "The test of life is to be found in the amount of pain one can absorb without spoiling joy."[1] And Archbishop Desmond Tutu describes joyous living (I paraphrase here) as an ability to be with suffering in such a way that it does not have the ultimate power to define our full existence.[2] The key is learning to hold both joy and suffering together, something that cannot be realized in isolation; it is rather made possible through others who model for us a possibility of transforming trauma that in turn enlarges our capacities to create and deepen love in the world.

Tending to trauma is bittersweet. On the one hand, there exists a deep anguish and pain that cannot and will not be overcome by willpower, a person's belief systems, cultural identity, or past experiences. Suffering from trauma runs so deep that we are never quite sure where all this will lead or whether we will ever feel whole again. On the other hand, in those moments where we find

Befriending the Tears

an affirmation of the preciousness of our lives during our suffering, we begin to see that no experience we go through can ever rob us of our ultimate identity in and as those who are beloved.

Trauma simply arrests us and returns us to our primordial experience of contingency. We are not infinite. We are not over or above anything. And somehow, with all of life in this mysterious experience, we are linked together. Then at the moment trauma occurs, we no longer can hide behind our social successes or status, or our material possessions. Somewhere hidden in the middle of our freefall, a sacred recognition of our being-ness unfolds beyond all labels or understandings. And when others greet us in that spirit, a presence of compassion and care, by a smile or even another's tears, we become awakened to the truth of who we really are and who we have always been; regardless of whether we have known it.

The timing around my accident was such that for a good portion of my following hospitalization, the nurses were on a week-long strike protesting for fair wages. Being committed to social justice, I was happy that this was taking place. But being a patient in desperate need, this heightened my uncertainty around the level of care I would receive each day. When strikes like this happen, I discovered, hospitals must contract outside nurses to fill in the gap. This means that those who fill in are likely unfamiliar with the systems they are thrust into. And this

Trauma and Renewal

creates barriers to fulfilling the basic nursing tasks and level of care required.

I remember feeling the anxiety of my pain deepened by fear with the likelihood I wouldn't receive compassionate care on any given day due to the strike. And in truth, during this time many of the care staff who showed up were undertrained and subpar, also failing in providing interculturally sensitive care, as they were not adequately briefed on patients under their care. While some of the nurses did their best to provide personalized care, the majority seemed overburdened, unprepared, and scattered.

But the presence of one nurse I met in this time still reverberates with me today.

Gerardo was a Latino Catholic nurse, and from the moment he walked in, I could feel a warmth of presence. As he looked into my eyes, telling me his name, I felt the warmth of his tone, which seemed to carry the tenderness of Mother Mary. He asked me in a soft voice, "What has happened?" I could feel that this question was asked with concern and not as merely routine. It was as if he was asking the question from an intimate knowledge of suffering himself. There was a disarming sincerity and genuine curiosity from him, which invited me to respond, expressing to him the level of pain I was in. After I shared this, I felt his utmost concern and willingness to do whatever was possible in his power to alleviate the pain. Sensing his mercy and care, I began to tell him more of my

Befriending the Tears

story. After a few moments of deep listening and compassionate witnessing, he showed affectionate regard to me and my words, responding, "I am so sorry this happened, I am here to do whatever I can to ease any suffering you may feel. You be sure to hit this button and call me with absolutely anything I can do to bring you comfort. If you need me to move your pillow, get you a snack to enjoy. Whatever it is, I will do my best to help."

He became an incarnate angelic presence to me that day, embodying the divine energies of compassion and presence, giving his all to meet another person in their worst moment. Although the interaction was brief, maybe five minutes, I felt as though he offered me a small, profound portion of eternal love. Moments in time like that can have a profound effect. Thanks to the way he treated me and showed interest in my well-being, I began to open myself to then finding compassion toward myself, toward my vulnerability. In that time, I began to learn one of life's most important lessons: Regardless of the state I find myself in, *I am infinitely cared for and loved.*

My awareness of being loved in my state of helplessness also significantly deepened through interactions I had with my parents. When I first was able to look into my mother's eyes, I could see both the heartbreak she was experiencing in the situation but also her relief that I was still alive. She embraced me with a love that echoes divine maternal qualities. After giving her an extended side hug from the bed, I looked up to see my father. And

Trauma and Renewal

within this moment, there was a quickening in me unlike anything I had ever experienced. For the first time in my life, I witnessed my father weep. Tears began to flow from his face and all the emotional distance I had felt growing up now seemed to dissolve.

The look on his face was a mixture of relief that I was alive and sorrow that his son was in such suffering. Despite my fear as to how others would see my new vulnerabilities, I felt like he saw my suffering and loved me anyway.

In the twenty-eight years of my life prior to that point, I had only one other memory of my father crying. But never like that. And strangely, seeing him weep and giving him a hug and feeling his love for me as his son, opened a portal of connection I never thought was possible. In that connection with him, I felt as though he could see me and also be with me in my place of weakness. This connection moved something within me, too, as though it was now time for me to also embrace places within myself I had suppressed and repressed for far too long. In my most torturous and pain-filled days, it was the little moments of compassion that seemed to help keep me alive.

Within the exchange with my parents, I was beginning to learn that my belovedness is not dependent upon my state of health or performance. Belovedness is beyond the roles we have learned to play or those we believe we have failed at; it is rather something extended to us freely through life itself and can even be awakened in us

70

Befriending the Tears

in moments of tremendous doubt and pain. We can only stumble into this gift, rather than acquire it through hard-fought discipline or any act of our ego. Because the gift of love is so disarming, it can only be received by those who are disarmed. And trauma is exactly that, something that breaks down any armor we have built up around ourselves. And we are simply left with an open wound; whether we choose to address it is up to us. If we can tend to it skillfully in relationship, the opening can also mysteriously be the place where we begin to be touched by a love that knows no end.

Although I had been a competitive collegiate athlete and dedicated my entire adolescence to athletics, I never felt at home in my body. I was filled with the desire to be a victorious conqueror. Training to be an athlete as a mixed-race male youth of color who is of Chinese–Malaysian–Mexican–American descent, often meant that I had to stretch and push my body beyond limits. Excessive force, willpower, and "mind over matter" attitudes were societally ingrained. Because I did not have the natural strength of others, I kept pushing my body to compete. I did not know how to love or respect my body.

Now I understand that I had internalized patriarchy and aspects of the theology I had grown up with, which had a lot to do with the way I viewed myself. Patriarchal portrayals in the media often showed star athletes who possessed superior physical strength and lacked any

Trauma and Renewal

weakness. Those transcendent figures provided images of success that I saw and aspired toward. "No pain, no gain," was a common refrain used in collegiate sports as a justification of impositional (and even violent) behavior toward myself rather than compassionate acceptance. All these sensibilities further displaced me from my own body, its rhythms and needs. So, when my accident happened, it was the first time I felt the importance of extending sensitivity toward my body, especially as it was a body fighting for its very life. I suddenly became aware of the deep limitations of and constraints on my body. I saw how hard my body would work on my behalf and for the first time ever, I began to appreciate the sacred gift of my embodied life.

Trauma is not something to be overcome through a mentality of conquest, but it can be transformed through mercy and compassion, which are borderless. As I extended sensitivity toward my body for the first time, I saw how prayer and meditation can be of such vital importance: not as a discipline or regimented manual for conquering trauma, but rather as a practice that (intentionally or unintentionally) supports us in entrusting our lives to a field of care and connection that is greater than ourselves, this greater network of relations that knows each of us as a part of a whole, and as inextricably woven to all life.

While I am sympathetic to intentional models of prayer that I and many grew up with, as a way of "casting

Befriending the Tears

our cares" and burdens unto God, I believe prayer and meditation can be practiced without belief in a greater supreme being. Prayer is simply any act of placing trust in the sacredness permeating life. Prayer is about entrusting the yearnings (great and small) of our lives to that which is beyond any one of us (yet present within all of us) and about discovering concrete assistance and care from others (whether visible, invisible, human, or more than human).

The many others who care for us could be understood as the "cloud of witnesses," which the author of the New Testament book of Hebrews refers to. When considered in relationship to trauma and posttraumatic growth, the "cloud of witnesses" includes the field of beings actively offering us love right in the middle of whatever trials and tribulations we walk through. And it is through giving ourselves to a great network of compassion that we may begin to find restoration and recovery beyond our efforts or strivings, slowly learning through that network to meet all the tender places of our lives with kindness.

Perhaps understanding the importance of prayer as a way of entrusting oneself to a greater field of relational care helps us to grasp why Jesus spent many nights in prayer as he suffered the ongoing nature of trauma as an oppressed person and why the night before he was executed, he prayed throughout the long night. And it also explains the distress he shared with his disciples,

Trauma and Renewal

when they were unable to stay awake with him and pray alongside him. Jesus who knew the power of relational healing was left to suffer alone.

The trauma of the cross came not only through the physical and psychological torment Jesus endured, but a large aspect of that trauma came through the spiritual and relational betrayal and abandonment by his closest friends and community. Ultimately, Jesus even felt the trauma reach its pinnacle, as he inquired why the divine presence was nowhere to be found as he expressed the anguish of betrayal crying out on the cross with a haunting question, *My God, my God, why have you forsaken me?*[3]

Our journey toward wholeness demands relational support. Our transformation becomes more possible in the presence of others who embody and reflect our belovedness to us—though depending on circumstances, the presence of those others who reflect back to us our divine preciousness may be easy or more difficult to find. Yet a presence of care and regard need not always be experienced through what is visible (although the material cannot be excluded from trauma transformation) nor does it need to be offered by someone we consider close to us (think of Gerardo, the Latino Catholic nurse), or even a trained "professional"; this can be a person who sees our suffering and moves closer anyway, without judgment or pretense. This person can

Befriending the Tears

only do this because they see within us that which is greater than the pain we carry. This presence can be in the form of community, it can be found in those who have passed on, whether we connect with them through their writings or ancestral practices from various cultural or spiritual traditions. And it can be found in the natural world whether through a sense of tenderness from a beloved animal, plant, or the divine, or cosmic being where we find ourselves in the presence of that which is simply with us compassionately in all our imperfections.

Certain intersections between trauma, the spiritual, the cultural, and the natural world hold that transformative presence. It is not our hard work that overcomes trauma but the way we entrust our lives to the presence of relational support and tenderness. And although we may not know the extent or the time frame of the process, we can trust this long and indefinite process when practiced in communion with these intersections of the spiritual, cultural, the natural, and in relationship with the entire cosmos. It's this spiritual communion I experienced in one of the most intense parts of my recovery that I'll write about in the next chapter, namely, a sixteen-hour mystical vision in which I found myself in the company of Jesus.

Trauma and Renewal

PERSONAL PRACTICE OF CONSCIOUS WAITING

1. Take a moment to pause and simply acknowledge your experience.
2. Breathe deeply.
3. Check in to your body scanning any sensations that may be present.
4. Notice if you can identify anything pleasant or new through your sense of sight or sound.
5. Extend gratitude for the experience of life's rhythms being experienced uniquely through you.
6. Allow yourself to savor this experience and rest in the gift extended toward you.

PART II

VISIONS

4

RADIATING LOVE

While the last part explored some of the ways trauma affects us in similar ways (despite our different circumstances around that trauma), there are other experiences in trauma or after trauma that occasionally arise and may support our ongoing healing. These differ from person to person. Not uncommon across the literature, research, and cultural histories are a variety of visionary experiences (coming through various means, including "altered states of consciousness" such as flow-states, meditation moments, dreams, ancestral connections, plant medicines, and near-death experiences) through which we confront the Ultimate.

We are all profoundly affected by traumatic events of our lives, and in some cases involving traumatic experiences, they are coupled with a liminality that gives us a sense of in-betweenness related to time and space, to what is internal and spiritual. Raising the connection between trauma and visionary experiences (and the potential wisdom therein) in no way justifies or romanticizes the grotesque reality of trauma; instead it notes this

Trauma and Renewal

potential connection that may additionally be before us when the undesirable unfolds.

Because of the ways trauma disrupts all that we "know," I would like to offer another way to think about the relationship between trauma and visionary experiences, with the goal of imagining how we might move closer to a reverence and sense of communion with the fullness of life rather than exclusion or superiority toward it. To do this, we should acknowledge two major factors that can help us to discern[1] how to integrate these altered states in our work with trauma.

The first is related to the fruit that comes from them: Are these experiences that make us more compassionate, open-hearted, present, and respectful of our embodied lives? Or do the altered states make us more afraid, avoidant, closed off, or create a sense of separateness (or even superiority or harsh judgment) from our very lives and the lives of others in the world? If the latter, this altered state may be a dangerously "spiritualized" way of justifying harm and violence. The second factor when considering these visionary experiences is related to the distinction between disassociation (which is characterized by being cut off from ourselves) and those life-affirming altered states of consciousness that grant us greater comfort and healing in the midst of (or after) trauma, states that support us in touching the wounds of our lives with greater sensitivity, protection, and respect.

Radiating Love

Historically, there are many occasions when contemplatives have found themselves in altered states of consciousness arising from great suffering, such as Teresa of Avila's multiple near-death experiences; or the story of Julian of Norwich, who, when she was profoundly ill and after receiving last rites, received a series of sixteen revelations; or Ignatius of Loyola, as he was recovering from injuries from military duty, awakened to a new way of nonviolence and psychospiritual practices called the examen, which created a profound spiritual path of attention and meditation for monastics and lay people through the centuries.

From a more secular standpoint, Carl Jung also affirmed the importance of dreams as that which we should be open to, analyze, and even uncover guidance from. Or the artist Matisse, as his health declined and limited mobility constrained him, found a creative flow state and visionary path, creating artworks differently than the paint and brush palettes, now painting on walls from his wheelchair, extending drawing and painting utensils by a long stick as well as developing cutouts/designs with scissors and colored paper. In other words, these "altered states" can become a bridge to re-creating and reorienting the suffering in our lives so that we can approach the suffering with greater care, courage, and connection.

With the hope that sharing my experience creates room for you to reconsider how the luminous aspects may be present for your journey in transforming trauma

Trauma and Renewal

or that of those you support, I would now like to share glimpses of my own personal visionary experiences received during an extensive surgery and the several days that followed. While you may or may not have gone through what you deem a visionary experience in the aftermath of trauma, it's important to widen our view of how elements of these occurrences can aid us or those we're in community with, in holistic efforts toward trauma transformation.

One way we can broaden our views on what counts as a visionary experience is to demystify our understanding. Often, these manifestations can be described in very lofty terms and unintentionally perpetuate a certain form of spiritual elitism. But as with the example of Matisse, they may be moments where we come to a kind of opening that birth new understandings about our personhood, our community, renewing ways in which we serve our communities. Other examples could be found in people like Rwandan humanitarian Maggy Barankitse, who was tied up and forced to watch the killing of her people and then to bury the dead. In her grief, she had a vision for creating places of refuge for displaced people, which became the beginning of the Maison Shalom organization. Another example comes from the stillness Howard Thurman writes of in his early encounter with Halley's Comet at the age of eleven as he witnessed its passing, suddenly anxious that the comet might fall on him. In his words he shares his mother's

Radiating Love

response to him and the effects it had: "'Nothing will happen to us, Howard. God will take care of us.' In that moment something was touched and kindled in me, a quiet reassurance that has never quite deserted me. As I look back on it, what I sensed then was the fact that what stirred in me was one with what created and controlled the comet. It was this inarticulate awareness that silenced my fear and stilled my panic."[2]

I hope that in sharing the visionary elements of the experiences above, we can see the vast diversity of what these experiences could look like as well as the ways in which they are inherently providing creative bridges to transform suffering rather than our getting stuck or drowning in our pain. In considering visionary experiences, we may begin to see how these visionary experiences can play a role in the transformation of trauma.

My intention in sharing this is not to create any exhaustive criteria for visionary experiences but to normalize their presence in our pursuit of wholeness and surface the gifts that these occurrences may be able to offer us if we are interested in spiritually integrative ways of tending trauma.

While the first eight days of my hospital stay were filled with dread and suffering, on day nine—October 25— things began to change. On this day I endured what I now call "the long surgery." Initially scheduled for eight hours, the surgery lasted nearly sixteen. And it was

Trauma and Renewal

during this extended surgery I experienced a profound spiritual awakening I can only describe as the liminal space between life and death. This was the beginning of deep change in my relationship to suffering.

Although I experienced the visions over six years ago, because of their lucidity, it feels like it happened yesterday.[3] As soon as I was sedated by anesthesia, I became alert and aware, very conscious of my present suffering. I knew I was in an operation and under tremendous pain with great fear about what might come next. In this state of my dismay, I noticed someone who appeared with plain clothing, olive skin, and of seemingly Middle Eastern descent. Immediately I could feel the warmth in the person's presence and I understood that person to be Jesus. Jesus radiated mercy, love, and dignity. As he walked toward me with a gentle kindness, boundless compassion, and eternal joy, I could sense in him that the wound in my leg did not cause him worry, and his sheer ability to connect to my suffering in love began to calm and ground me. I could sense his love for me was immeasurable and without judgment. In my woundedness I felt completely and radically accepted. This was a moment in which I knew I was infinitely and irrevocably cared for.

In the comfort of Jesus's presence, I began to tell him what happened to my leg and about the accident that had almost cost me my life. I told him how concerned I was for my family. He listened with attentiveness, patient

Radiating Love

understanding, and without interrupting. I can only describe his way of listening as that of a most dear friend accompanying me through it all.

After I finished talking, he reached toward me to the place where the most immediate pain was felt (my open wound) and began to offer healing touch and energy. He moved slowly and with extraordinary diligence, mindfulness, and intention. The sensitivity with which Jesus touched my suffering, I sensed, could have only been explained by his knowing suffering intimately himself. But it was not only that he knew the depths of suffering, it was also as if he knew there was a hidden wholeness present, too.

Because my wounds were so tender, open, and persistent, Jesus moved with gentleness, courage, and caution, which was noticeable to me. Jesus's pacing was different from what I had habitually been accustomed to as I was well trained in efficiency, productivity, and moving expediently. Jesus's behavior demonstrated to me the importance of the small things, the subtle and slower things, and a way of relating to each aspect of reality with an eternal quality of love.

While I felt humiliated to be so exposed and meet Jesus in such a wounded state, he treated me as if I were the most precious person in the world. Jesus welcomed and embraced all of me. I realized through this intervention that my leg was beginning to regain strength. As my leg was recovering, I then started to become aware of

Trauma and Renewal

deeper layers of suffering I was holding that had to do with matters of my own heart.

It became apparent that I was still holding on to bitterness, regret, shame, and fear. It was as though I believed there were areas of my life that were beyond love's reach, making me unworthy of care. But now I began to feel myself being somehow safe enough to be more honest about aspects of my life that I previously worked hard to avoid, dismiss, or cover up.

It was during this compassionate exchange with Jesus that I began to be fully and radically honest with myself, my life up until that point, and all the healing I truly desired, which went far beyond my wounded leg. Struggles I had with insecurity, honesty about my pain, addictive behaviors, and the cycles of shame surfaced in this time, along with my belief that I needed to carry the burdens of my life alone. Due to the internalized voice of self-hatred, I had developed a pattern of making decisions that were selfish and ultimately hurt those whom I loved the most, starting with my spouse, my children, but also my extended family. In this part of the vision, I began to feel the suffering my actions caused, the weightiness of the harm I caused others. I knew that I wanted to make things right, but doing so felt like an impossibility on my own.

I then began to feel the healing Jesus offered me was not contingent upon my own abilities nor limited to my leg but was to be extended to the entirety of my being.

Radiating Love

I began to experientially know that wholeness includes every aspect of experience, body, mind, spirit. Past, present, and future. All my life was known and held and loved. I learned here that wholeness is not the absence of imperfections or suffering, but rather a way of being in loving relationship with all that we are tempted to reject.

Jesus was inviting me to start anew in relationship to myself and all the things I despised about myself. My internalized self-judgments, including self-rejection, self-loathing, and self-hatred, were not the final truth about me, I could welcome those places inside me with a love that went far beyond them.

With Jesus's support and presence, I noticed my perspective on my own suffering began to change. I perceived that love was not conditional and did not require any absence of vulnerability, but rather it simply called me to extend compassion toward the entirety of my experience.

I could sense that Jesus was able to perceive my life in a way that was far more life-affirming than anything I could see for myself. I then asked Jesus if he was able to help me see myself in that same compassionate way he saw me. If it were to be possible, I confessed, then I would need new eyes because I felt mine had been stained, unable to perceive the all-encompassing love.

With great generosity, he reached toward his own eyes and grabbed them, taking them out and then placed his eyes where mine had been. It was such a strange,

Trauma and Renewal

awkward, and healing experience all at once. When I received his eyes, everything I saw became new. I began to see millions of pixels of light that seemed to shine forth the wonder, brilliance, and splendor of life. With Jesus's vision, there was much more expansiveness, clarity, and wonder in all of life.

Because at the time I had been studying the ways our brains can change through spiritual practice, I then also asked Jesus if he could help rewrite my neural pathways. I told him that my current neural pathways were stuck in entrenched patterns, but I longed to have them reconfigured[4] so that truth could flow more easily, and so I could engage my life and the world more compassionately.

At my request, Jesus obliged and began to open my brain and touch the grooves of it, reshaping all those places that had enslaved and oppressed me. I can only describe this experience as one of intense comfort and as a transformation of the deepest sort. Through this deep work, I sensed a profound renewal in every area inside me where the life-shattering problems that were weighing me down seemed so small in comparison to the love, truth, and care that was present. And it was through the gift of Jesus's work on my physical, emotional, and spiritual life that I now felt empowered to begin a process of making amends with those whom I loved.

In this aura of wholeness, I began to feel my entire being raised to life. I then felt inclined to ask Jesus explicitly, "What, exactly, happened during my

Radiating Love

accident?" In "real" time, all I could remember is that it happened so fast. I had no clue of who hit me and how I went down. I only recall being left for dead in the middle of the road in excruciating pain.

In response to my question, I was taken back to the scene of the accident and could watch it as if it were being played as a movie. I observed myself riding freely and joyously down the road and then witnessed the truck that came out of nowhere and suddenly crashed into my bike. I then saw myself being hurled to the ground, but what was different about this showing was the presence of three divine beings who appeared and came to my side as soon as I was hit.

They seemed to carry me as I was launched off my bike and they then set me down softly on the road. I was amazed by this scene because in the moment of the accident, it did not seem gentle at all. It was even more shocking because the way these angelic beings held me and laid me down was with the tenderness of a mother who would gently lay down a newborn to sleep at night. In this vision there was a sense that I was deeply cared for, held, and attended to in my very worst moments. Even then, I was not alone, and there was care being extended unto me.

After this portion of the vision ended, I felt undeniably that while this vision was given to me, its insights were universal and that even amid the unthinkable and even when we do not sense, perceive, or experience it consciously, there is a divine dimension at work.

Trauma and Renewal

Even though I grew up as a Pentecostal Christian with openness toward supernatural visions and experiences, if you would have asked me what I thought about mystical experiences such as the one I just described, I would have listened with a lot of skepticism. That may be your response as well. But my hope is in looking at trauma and healing, that an openness to insights or visions that come in our times of trauma might allow us to see what we might not have been able to perceive, receive, or accept before. Trauma, by opening liminal space, is its own unique invitation to seeing our lives, our loves, our losses, our wounds differently.

And while the visions I experienced were not entirely pleasant by any means and involved very difficult edges to them, they seemed to me to be aligned with what have long been understood across many different traditions as visions, which are among a set of experiences which help us reconcile our past, present, and future.

Visionary experiences present along a wide range. Some are more ecstatic, but there are also visionary experiences that come about in the most ordinary of circumstances when we are not looking for them at all, or attempting to imagine anything along the lines of what Carl Jung called our own self-understanding.[5] Take Thomas Merton's revelation on Fourth and Walnut,[6] where he perceived everyone at the intersection "shining like the sun," or Sitting Bull's prophetic vision about the impending attack on his tribe.[7] We also might imagine

Radiating Love

a moment of deep connection with others around a dinner table, creating art, singing songs, or even dancing together. These are the visionary experiences that bring us into a greater sense of relationship with ourselves and the rest of the world.

What all visionary moments share are the diverse ways they can aid us in reweaving threads of the seeming fragments of our lives. And if we understand visions as carrying potentially reconciling resources, they also can hold profound possibilities for integration, being especially helpful when we feel mired in the present moment of unrelenting suffering.

We return to our earlier question: How can we discern what visions may be life affirming rather than those that are spiritually destructive? While there is no one sufficient answer to this question, I believe a major criterion lies in how a spiritual experience or dream or vision leads us toward generative possibilities, honoring relationships, and creative agency rather than isolation, despair, self-criticism, or fear. In my case, even including the most troubling aspects of the vision, in its entirety it was geared toward extending loving-kindness toward my experience, toward empowerment toward a growing desire to restore relationships, and toward a clarity related to the sanctity of life.

In many traditions, working with visions requires a trustworthy guide or elder. In my case, there were many different spiritual guides I could name who were

Trauma and Renewal

resources for me in the immediate days after my long surgery. The first was James Finley. I listened to his audio teachings[8] on trauma and spirituality over and over in hopes that I would find comfort on the long road of healing. Second, was the guide of the vision itself. My experience of the vision was so deeply transformative precisely because of the sense of being deeply understood, loved, and led by the presence of Jesus who was with me. Though I preached many sermons about Jesus long before this vision, I was stunned at this new understanding of how deeply he saw and met my suffering and was not afraid of it. Jesus did not run from my suffering or seek to minimize it in any way, but rather made himself available to be with me in my situation and in my pain, offering positive regard each step of the way. While I never consciously called to Jesus during the vision (he simply appeared to me and approached me with compassion), his presence throughout made all the difference in guiding me through my suffering.

I have since reflected upon the unrelenting love that Jesus showed to me and wondered *how* this was possible. This led me to recounting the great suffering he himself endured in his life. While the passion of Christ has been well documented, Jesus's experiences of trauma were lifelong. Jesus's family of origin was familiar with the intergenerational trauma of poverty, coupled with the fact that he was born during a period of mass genocide against newborns among his people. Additionally, Jesus

Radiating Love

was born under abysmal and inhumane conditions without health care provided for his mother.

As a Jewish man, Jesus also knew cultural trauma. He was a member of the "disinherited" and ethnically oppressed peoples living under the Roman Empire in ancient Palestine. Jesus knew emotional trauma: He was nearly murdered in his hometown when he preached his inaugural sermon. After that he survived forty days of fasting and temptation in the wilderness, where ministering angels kept him alive. Later in his ministry he knew institutional trauma. "The son of man has no place to lay his head," he stated.

And on the night before he died, he went through a trauma of betrayal. This was intensified as his closest friends and companions scattered, leaving him, denying him, and those near him, when he asked them to stay awake in prayer with him, were unable to keep awake with him on the eve of his death.

And we know that after Jesus was taken by the authorities, he experienced the slow and tormenting physical trauma as his body was humiliated and tortured. He was whipped, beaten, spit on, and a victim of extreme violence. His body was so weakened that he was unable to carry his cross by himself, requiring the accompaniment of another to walk the cross to Golgotha.

On the cross, he died the slow and agonizing death of asphyxiation. Ultimately, the epitome of this spiritual trauma is evident in his experience of the abandonment

Trauma and Renewal

of the divine presence during the last moments of life as he was being crucified.

Up until that point, he was experientially intimate with the divine presence, referring to the sacred as Abba or loving parent. Yet in this all-time low on the cross, Jesus cried out his trauma experience with the following words: God, why have you forsaken me? His last breath was taken from him by unbearable forces of oppression. For those who understand so many of the forms of trauma, it is clear that we cannot understand Jesus's life, ministry, or healing ministry without also understanding the severe trauma he endured.[9]

Connecting to a spiritual guide such as Jesus in my vision was profoundly important to and supportive for me. And connecting with spiritual guides was one of Jesus's own practices and one we witness in the Mount of Transfiguration where he convened with Moses and Elijah to receive wisdom and strength for his impending death. And through that story, we see that it is not only Jesus who is a trustworthy spiritual guide when it comes to suffering, but other wisdom beings from other generations and traditions who embody love and healing and the desire for our holistic and collective flourishing.

In other cultural and spiritual traditions, many spiritual guides come in feminine forms. Examples that come to mind are Shekinah, Devaki, Sophia, Majka, and another—very important to me as an Asian American—Guanyin. Guanyin is known as a bodhisattva

Radiating Love

of compassion and a being who has consciously devoted herself to deny personal nirvana, instead availing herself to extend compassion to all sentient beings. Not only is Guanyin important to me due to my own cultural heritage but also in the way she embodies an alternative to the idealized comfort and success-driven society glorified in modern North American culture. Guanyin reveals that spiritual depth and power is not found in the absence of avoidance of suffering but in the ability to ever return toward transforming it through the power of compassion.

Wisdom can come from many diverse places, and there are many guides who are available to walk with us in this great work. The power of the guide lies in the kind of life they have lived and the suffering they have intimately walked with. It's less important who the guide is than that there is the building of an authentic personal relationship with the guide in order to entrust ourselves to learn from their presence and receive their compassionate support.

If we ever find ourselves seemingly lost, it is good to know in our time of need that there are other wise beings who are ready and willing to help us find our way back home to ourselves.

Another key element that can help in discerning our visions is having nonjudgmental listeners with whom you can share your experience, who will not discount it or write it off. While this option may not always be

Trauma and Renewal

available (especially for those whom the world consistently marginalizes based on their identities), it is important for the full integration of the vision received. Many health care systems do not create intentional ways to listen and witness the various ruminations that occur in the trauma recovery journey, but it is vital that those who endure them have a space to share these journeys honestly and in loving community. Thankfully, I was able to share these experiences with my family and even a few friends who listened with kindness.

AMOS'S REFLECTION

It was during those earlier weeks, especially in the evenings, that I dimly recalled his visions. The dimness has to do with my memory as set next to the vividness of what Aizaiah described seeing. He described seeing dynamic lights, bright colors, and Jesus. "Do you see that, dad?" he would repeatedly ask. "What, son?" I would wonder. "The lights …, the bright lights …, there, and there, and there." I would then follow his gestures and pointings. This happened over two or three nights, particularly after one or two of the most intense and extended surgeries, with their radiance and luster waxing and waning, or their aggregations shifting from one part of the room, to another, then to one corner of the ceiling, and after to the other corner from his bed, etc. I would listen to my son, mostly, without much to add by way of response, if I remember correctly. I don't believe I was discouraging his sharing, although I was not encouraging either.

Radiating Love

As a Pentecostal preacher's kid and Pentecostal missionary kid myself, and a recognized Pentecostal theologian, I had a range of mixed emotions to Aizaiah's visions. On the one hand, why would not the Lord be giving our son these visions of light and love? Pentecostals expect dreams and visions, or, to use more psychologically inflected (if not loaded) notions, dissociative states or alternative states of consciousness might well be means through which the Holy Spirit might be speaking to us.

Aizaiah's own studies and coursework had introduced him to internal family systems (IFS) theory and to compassion practice, and prior to his accident, he had begun to not only share insights from these segments of his study with me and his mother but also invited me to explore, via IFS methods, the complexities of my own journey, in particular to begin having self-compassion (something I am still working on). All of this was consistent, then, with how the accident slowed Aizaiah down enough to open him up to portals of divine communication, similar to the heavenly ladders and angelic hosts that appeared for patriarchs of ancient Israel, Jacob, for instance. Through these portals vocational invitations were extended that the patriarch would catalyze, thus guiding a lifelong commitment. So, the lights, their flickering, were all prompts that gathered the attention, inviting clarification that, as expected in Pentecostal-charismatic spirituality, would unfold over the course of obedient response to what we knew.

On the other hand, having been a kind of interdisciplinary theologian for a bit as well, I knew enough lay psychology to expect that not only the trauma of the accident but the possible side effects of drugs and multiple extensive surgeries—this one stretching over sixteen hours—and such "visions," like REM-dreaming or lucid-dreaming, are ways in which our subconscious responds to what has just happened, in order to enable renewal for what needs to be navigated tomorrow, and the next day.

To be sure, within a naturalistic frame, then, these are more projections of our psyche rather than divine communications. Yet Aizaiah was not—at least I neither felt nor wished he was—asking for my analyses of what he was seeing and sharing. And in the end, however, I also did not see any inconsistency between these experiences being naturally induced, on the one hand, and with their also being deployed for divine and vocational purposes. In fact, my own theology of divine action in the created and human world presumed this kind of supervening overlay between what happens in our minds and bodies (in our material world), on the one side, with how God "acts" through these creaturely and cosmic realities, on the other side. This also enabled me to simply accompany my son along this journey, appreciating what he saw and shared, but even then, not sufficiently taken up with these due to my own perspectives and questions about his experience.

I am grateful for my father's response to lovingly bear witness to what was happening to me. Although he had a background in Pentecostal visions and felt an internal

Radiating Love

skepticism toward my own visions, he did not shame me or speak ill of my experience and that was very important.

And here is where the power of trauma companions is vital, whether they be doctors, nurses, chaplains, religious leaders, family, friends, and/or spiritual directors. How we respond to others who encounter dreams or visions that may sound strange to our logical mind is so important. The call to those who listen is to develop compassionate awareness of nonjudgmental and deep listening where a person who is traversing the intensity of suffering can be honest about the experience. We do not need to understand everything about what is happening (much less *why*) when these visions are given, but we can hold space for others as they navigate an experience of being broken open by love.

Further, if a vision is not one that appears to be life-affirming, it is crucial that trauma companions inquire of those we journey with, what life-affirming actions may be taken in our shown support. Supportive actions will vary from person to person and moment to moment but involve the whole person, including but not limited to their physical body, their emotional life, their cultural stories, as well as their spiritual longings.

Ultimately, I am suggesting that visions and/or mystical experiences can be transformative vehicles when they are guided by beings animated by love and shared in loving community (including those wisdom beings who

Trauma and Renewal

are not alive today). And through support we find new ways to integrate aspects of our experience we previously thought were excluded from love. We know the truth of the wisdom our visions share by how they call us to live with greater acceptance, humility, and harmony with ourselves and all others. Our trauma transformation is not only about us but about our pursuit of wholeness, which involves all those aspects that we are inclined to keep fragmented, as we bring them back into loving connection and relationship.

A PRACTICE OF CONNECTING TO A SPIRITUAL GUIDE

1. Identify a spiritual guide that you feel exudes the highest truth, compassion, and wisdom.
2. Ask them to connect with you in a way you might recognize and experience as life-affirming. And express to them your desire to learn from that guide how you might follow love's deepest reality.
3. You might ask for wisdom around a particular topic or note some aspect of your life in which you would like to live with greater freedom and wisdom. Or it may be just something open ended, where you express gratitude for any gifts or insights they might offer to you.
4. Make space and dedicated time, perhaps extended time, for this request. And in this time remain open and incline your ear to keep listening deeply.
5. After that dedicated time, in a notebook or journal, write down your conversation, what you observed, and how you felt.

Radiating Love

6. Reflect on how your body responded to this time, and how your body feels now, after that engagement. Perhaps relaxed, receptive, alive, or some other body response?
7. As you close the time, extend gratitude to the guide for any insights or graces experienced.
8. As you move into your day, you may not feel the need to act in any way in response to this time, but you might find it helpful to take a concrete action based in insights from that engagement. Concrete actions in response can help ground the wisdom you received deeper into your daily life.

5

EXPERIENCING ALIVENESS

Personal healing is intimately linked with the healing of the Whole. Each time we reconcile fragments within ourselves and reconcile our own stories, new pathways of wholeness are created so that all can benefit. For those who have insights, visions, or other profound experiences of transformation, there is in an invitation to realize that insights we receive are intended to offer nourishment to the entire world.

However, this link between the personal and the Whole is subtle and not always easily named or understood. It is especially important that in sharing our own journey of trauma transformation, we receive insights as gifts, letting go of any savior complex or attitudes that place us above others. In other words, our collective healing does not come as a new and improved "to-do list" or ego-project. While each of us have important stories to share, the medicine is in the sharing with others, creating spaces in ourselves for greater compassion and care. Wholeness is about the ways in which we continue

Experiencing Aliveness

to show up in our humanity, offer the gifts where we can, and humbly receive from so many others along the way. We are all on the journey together.

After I experienced the personal healing I shared in the previous chapter, the vision continued as I now found myself with more to learn from Jesus. He invited me first to a walk and then to journey with him through his public ministry. Though I had read through the gospels many times prior to this vision and thought I was familiar with Jesus's life, what I encountered in this journey together exceeded all my previous understandings. What follows in this chapter, is my retelling of this long vision where I was accompanied by Jesus in a period of contemplation.

In the vision and in the initial moments after I received such powerful personal healing from Jesus, I began to have full confidence in my own journey toward wholeness. And in this naivete I felt newfound energy to go out and evangelize, to "save" the world from all of its suffering. It obviously did not take long for old thinking patterns and habits of ministry to return. As a well-trained Protestant Christian, I reasonably assumed my primary task was to be of service to others (forgetting about myself in the process). I assumed that I had now spent enough time being cared for, and now it was time to offer the same to others. I turned to Jesus and asked,

103

Trauma and Renewal

"So where shall we begin the healing work?" Jesus smiled and offered a gentle but subversive reply, "Come with me, let's go take a walk for a bit."

A walk? I thought to myself, puzzled by Jesus's response. *There are ongoing global wars, problems of poverty, racism, sexism, classism, and an ecological catastrophe!* And here (in Jesus) was someone who could help, who knew the truth, and was a living embodiment of another way of being, beyond violence. Here was a person who knew suffering and how to transform it—and he wanted to take a stroll? I was confused by this, but knowing he was the wisdom teacher, I was afraid to look foolish. I shrugged nonchalantly, "Sure, a walk sounds nice."

As we began our walk, I noticed the sun beginning to rise and the smell of mother earth. I had no idea where we were, where we were going, or what our purpose was. But I did notice that Jesus was walking in a calm, present, and patient manner. I could tell he was truly enjoying the experience, connecting in wonder, and as if the world were already whole.

I did my best to act normal and try not to show my anxiety about the state of the world. Everything he did and spoke of reflected amazement and enjoyment. I quietly wondered to myself if our enjoyment was an escape from the "real world." It also struck me that perhaps Jesus was experiencing the "real world" in a fullness that I had not yet been able to cultivate. He was of course my teacher, after all.

Experiencing Aliveness

While I was grateful for the serenity that Jesus seemed to be abiding in, I continued to wonder, "What joy is this man seeing?" and "How is he able to hold both suffering and joy together?" And it was during this walk where I began to learn from Jesus about taking delight in the ordinariness and simplicity of the human experience. The way he walked and talked with me was an invitation to come and taste the fullness that is readily available. It was an invitation to abide in love.

In the Gospel of John, Jesus extends an invitation for his followers to rest and abide in love. To teach them about this, Jesus uses a metaphor of the vine and branches. Jesus describes how the purpose of the branches is to bear fruit, and even those branches that bear fruit will be pruned and go through loss that they might bear even more fruit. Jesus concludes the parable stating that when a person abides in ultimate love, the true fruit is joy that is complete. It is not a joy that is conditional upon favorable circumstances, but rather a joy that comes from being with life as it is and is sustained in reciprocity. True abiding allows us to transcend the small stories we tell ourselves about what all this means (without being dismissive) as we hold both suffering and joy together in love.

It was on this walk with Jesus, I began to experientially learn about the wholeness that is lived through sincerity and simplicity.

Trauma and Renewal

I had no idea where Jesus was leading me (and perhaps he did not either!), but after walking together for some time we found a place to sit next to one another alongside a riverbank. It was a beautiful setting: calm, vital, and renewing. Rivers are present in the highest mountains and the lowest valleys, bodies of water that in many traditions connect the heavens and earth. I continued to wonder *why* we were here and *what* we were supposed to be doing. Jesus gave me no instruction. He simply began to meditate in silence.

While I was out of my comfort zone, I reminded myself that he was the wise guide, and I was the student. I clumsily tried to imitate his posture and act like I knew what it was that we were doing there. After a few minutes of stress, I was calmed by experiencing the presence of Jesus who was at ease and with no agenda. After repeated attempts to imitate the practice, I finally allowed myself to sink into my body and just be.

I then noticed the simplicity of beauty and the rhythms of life that were both still and always at work. I could feel the warmth of the sun, hear the water running, sense the wind on my back and face, and intuit the steady and ever-present sustaining force of life, which is constantly on the move and renewing the Whole. Next, I transitioned from a more conscious state of reflection to a wordless and thoughtless existence. Even the subjective nature of experience itself seemed to fade away. Time disappeared and there was only complete

Experiencing Aliveness

communion with the Whole. I no longer experienced linear progression or any sense of individuation, but rather a unity with the rhythms of love welling up in and as life itself.

And though I felt like we had just begun, I glanced around and noticed that the sun was beginning to set, the time of contemplation was coming to an end. I felt an overwhelming and peaceful restfulness that I had never known. It was as if all the burdens I was carrying were completely removed and life was light and free. As I reconnected with my body, I began to feel brand new. It was as if the healing journey I was on took another turn of deepening and expanding.

I turned to Jesus and asked, "What just happened? How could we have spent the whole day here? It felt like minutes!"

He replied simply and wisely: "It has been a while since you have taken time to just be." It was as if all that I longed for was not found in a certain condition or consciousness, but rather was always there quietly giving itself away to me and all things. I had nothing to do, nothing to perform, and the gift was found in allowing myself to rest in life itself.

Ancient East Asian wisdom is also derived from experiences at a river. The Yijing, which is translated in English as the Book of Changes, was composed by wise sages who spent time observing the patterns of life at a riverbank.[1]

Trauma and Renewal

They concluded that life itself is not one thing or another but involves interrelatedness, dynamism, and creative action. While the Yijing never articulates *rest* as the Christian tradition does, the wisdom offered is one that is cosmically embodied and in relationship to the Whole.

Additionally, many Indigenous communities throughout the world describe the more than human life as kin and relatives that we can listen to, understand, and be in reciprocal relationship with just as we would with another human. Raimon Panikkar, a scholar of comparative religion, describes a way of knowing in congruence with these alternative wisdoms, which are nature-based and relational. Panikkar calls this wisdom ecosophy.[2] He distinguishes ecosophy from ecology (which is distant, differentiated, and often experimental), and describes ecosophy as arising from deep listening to the earth on her own terms and for her own benefits. He says it is not wisdom *about* the earth but the wisdom *of* the earth.

When it comes to transforming trauma, returning to the wisdom that comes from nature-based traditions around the world can be liberating. In nature, we learn to discover the truth about the depths of our own lives that are often fragmented by our rationalist and overly individualistic ways of thinking. As we do, we may even begin to sense the rhythms of nature and how that is connected to our longings for realizing a more expansive wholeness.

Experiencing Aliveness

After the full day I spent with Jesus at the river, the vision with Jesus now changed, as I began to accompany him as he ministered and touched people from all backgrounds and experiences. I saw so many who were outcast, hurting, psychologically tormented, and spiritually traumatized. The intensity of Jesus's lived experience gave rise to the strength of his compassion.

And it was revealing to me that there were many whom Jesus did not heal and who did not seem to be transformed much by him. Yet in every occurrence of healing I did see, I noticed a common denominator: the connection to Jesus's blood. The blood of Jesus was real, material, and a spiritual source at the same time. Jesus's blood was a bridge unto others so that they may find renewal and restoration. Jesus's blood was a material, sacred, and conscious source of far-reaching and boundless compassion that emanates from Godself. Jesus gave himself entirely to love so that his entire being would become sustenance and renewal to all of life.

The great mystic and Catholic saint, St. Catherine of Siena once described the blood of Jesus as the way to truth and life abundant. Writing to her confessor, Blessed Raymond of Capua, she said, "I desire to see you inflamed and drowned in his sweetest blood, blended with the fire of his most ardent charity."[3] For St. Catherine, the blood of Jesus was the source from which all sweetness of love emerges, beckoning us toward transformation and wholeness. The blood of Christ restores

Trauma and Renewal

and renews all the hurting places within our lives and empowers us to care with eternal compassion. For St. Catherine, what we thought was going to destroy us becomes a potential opportunity for the divine glory to be newly expressed.

In this vision, after seeing countless miracles and healings performed by Jesus, the moment came for me to witness his passion and death. It was a dark day to see him undergo a suffering beyond description or understanding. In this vision, I felt the palpability of his fidelity to love without any exceptions. He refused to otherize in a radical way and seemed to hold all in a trust that love was grounded in ultimate reality. I could only weep as I watched him endure the trauma.

I witnessed him struggle until his last breath, giving his entire being to life even when love appeared nowhere to be found. And then he died.

In the vision, I was then suddenly near his body in the tomb where he was buried and saw his body lying there. There was no sound, utter silence, and nothingness.

The void was abyss-like, and I felt overcome by the vast darkness. It was a peculiar darkness that did not evoke fear but rather an unintelligible aspect of life that is nevertheless integral to the Whole. In this awareness, I felt as though nothing was to be rejected or excluded from participation in the Whole. Not even death.

Experiencing Aliveness

In this darkness I attempted to open myself to experience and trust, accepting the scene in front of me as fully as I could.

A bit later, I saw that where the tomb's entrance had once been covered, now the boulder that had covered the tomb was moved to the side. A great shining light pierced through the burial space where Jesus had been laid, but he was nowhere to be found. Only his shroud was left.

I walked outside and saw that it was a beautiful sunny day, calm and vibrant. It was a complete shift from the arresting darkness of the tomb. I then started to search for the resurrected Jesus. I stayed with the group of other followers. *Jesus must be alive,* I thought. *But where is he?* Suddenly and to my astonishment, I realized that the resurrected Christ was already there among us! I did not notice him because he appeared to have so much in common with the rest of the group. The only things making him recognizable were his scars, but they were not immediately evident, not as though the resurrected Christ had lost all connection to suffering, but rather as if the love that he embodied now shone through, more transparent, powerful, and possessing a glory unlike before.

Looking at every scar on his body verified to me that it was not only Jesus but that through the scars I observed, the revelation of eternal love was now even more clear. I recall the sense that love has been, is, and will be always there at each step of the way—that love

Trauma and Renewal

is the only everlasting reality. Through this encounter I knew assuredly that every one of us is infinitely loved by God through and through and through and through. It was after some moments with the resurrected Christ that I now began to reawaken to my own scars. I emerged from my surgery, finding myself aware and back in the operating room.

It was quite a shock to my system to awaken from surgery. Not least because I had just felt the intimate reality of Jesus being in friendship with me, but I was now informed by the nurses that the surgery was over, and I must now complete further tests. I could tell in their apprehension that I was still in serious condition, in recovery, so my first inclination was to ask the doctors how the procedure went and if I was going to be okay. One of the surgeons replied that everything looked good, but I needed to go to a recovery room.

As I was taken from the room, every bump and turn was brutal, and I was handled roughly, with disregard. When we finally arrived at the basement floor, I was deeply troubled by the way I was carelessly tossed from one bed to another—after coming from a vision where my life was held with the utmost care and compassion. I began to feel nauseous and extremely thirsty, even as I could taste only blood in the back of my throat. I felt as though I was beginning to suffocate and struggled for breath. I told the care team I felt as though I was dying and needed water. "It is not time for that, and

Experiencing Aliveness

you need to be still if you want this to end." I felt discounted, minimized, and confused by the inhumane treatment. Why was their agenda more important than my suffering?

I then wondered to myself, *Is this it? Am I now going to finally die?* Then I remembered how Jesus struggled in the moments before his death on the cross: thirsty and with great difficulty in breathing. I recalled and repeated Jesus's prayer within myself: "Father, into thy hands I commit my spirit," thinking this might mean the end of my life. But as soon as I finished the prayer, my struggles instantly dissipated. And I fell asleep.

In reflecting upon my vision of being with Jesus and the subsequent experience of surfacing from the vision, it seemed I was traversing in the liminality between life and death. Going through the struggle after surgery made me conscious that life is not ultimately happening on our terms, efforts, or willpower alone. Neither can any of our efforts prevent us from death. So, what shall our response be when life happens in ways we are not prepared for or in ways that we cannot anticipate? Do we attempt to fight back? Do we continue to resist death? What about when that fails?

There is nothing we must do; but we need not worry. We can instead entrust our lives into the Whole which is beyond both life and death. Entrusting ourselves to the Whole is not a stance of passivity or of allowing oneself

Trauma and Renewal

to be taken advantage of; rather it is the recognition that our redemption is not bound or conditional upon any finite circumstance.

When it comes to transforming trauma in community, this means that we are called to support each other in the ever-slow process of learning to trust a bit more with each breath. We all must pass through the gates of life and death (and perhaps life again) to the beyond, and we must do so personally. No one can do this for us; yet we find comfort knowing we are all finding our way through all of this together. And furthermore, our journey can be greatly enhanced when there are others who show up for us during our learning to trust, and who treat us with dignity, mercy, and compassion.

Final liberation does not lie in our ability to avoid death (though it is advisable that we do all we can to stop suffering and resist violence in any way possible) but lies in our capacity to entrust our lives to the Ultimate even when there are no options left. In the presence of deep suffering, we find that we must all personally find our way to cross the threshold. None of us is exempt, but we can find greater courage in the presence of others who are open to this mystery. And all of this reflects the divine presence already at work in all things, calling us to return home to ourselves and to rest in communion with all life.

Experiencing Aliveness

RELATIONAL PRACTICE WITH RUNNING WATER

1. Find a place in nature or in your own setting where water is flowing. If there is no place nearby, you may want to find a virtual place, perhaps listening to nature and water sounds online.
2. As you watch and/or listen to the sound of the water, honor the water for the gifts it brings.
3. Ask yourself what areas of your life could use a flow of renewal and replenishment.
4. Ask yourself what areas of life could be cleansed and transformed by the presence of water.
5. Prepare a drink of water and invite the flowing waters of life to bring you vitality and healing.
6. Entrust your life to the flow of the Whole and commit to allowing life to do what it will through you.

6

EVERY BEING BELONGS

In my own experience of the transformation of personal trauma I have grown in my understanding that our healing from trauma is woven together, communal. Indigenous and Aboriginal activist Lilla Watson said, in concert with her community, "If you have come here to help me you are wasting your time, but if you have come because your liberation is bound up with mine, then let us work together."[1] Within the wider Internal Family Systems (IFS) trainer community, there is a common phrase often repeated that speaks to how our wholeness is intimately related: "Self begets Self." Self is that eternal quality at the depth dimension of each being that holds wise healing capacities. When we relate to ourselves and one another from "Self," it unlocks more potent capacities of Self in others, and the momentum of healing builds. In other words, when a person is animated and guided by the grace of Self within, it not only comforts us internally but often disarms the walls and barriers that others place around it. IFS practitioners believe this is possible because, regardless of how distant a person

Every Being Belongs

may feel from Self, it is always there deep within and can never be damaged no matter the trauma one has lived through. And, because Self exists within each of us, no one person controls or owns the Self, even as it is always available to us.

While it may be comforting to know that each person carries the presence and power of Self within, that Self exists and deepens through our engagement with other-than-human life, too. Like the vision I experienced, being in nature's unadulterated grandeur, away from the capitalistic and extractive damages allowed me to experience a healing quality that gave rise to a song about freedom, justice, and liberation. Seeing my (then) two children with me in that setting also showed me how that which gave rise to a power within them also had capacity to usher wholeness into the world. Ultimately, the Self is most deeply realized and expanded through our relationships with one another.

Self is not only present within a person but a dimension inherent in us of all reality, which can never really be lost, even if it's buried and glossed over due to our petty preoccupations. This belief that all beings sharing in "Self" is something Thomas Merton also reflected on: "The more we persist in misunderstanding the phenomena of life, the more we analyze them out into strange finalities and complex purposes of our own, the more we involve ourselves in sadness, absurdity and despair. But it does not matter much, because no despair of ours can alter

Trauma and Renewal

the reality of things; or stain the joy of the cosmic dance which is always there. Indeed, we are in the midst of it, and it is in the midst of us, for it beats in our very blood, whether we want it to or not."[2]

The real secret is in intentionally letting go of all that hinders us from listening to this *cosmic dance* and in promoting ways of living that are nonviolent, spacious, and deeply respectful of life in all its forms. Trauma is not just something we experience as humans but is also present throughout the natural, living world, and it can be restored when we show up for one another in community.

In the 48 hours after my life-threatening procedure, as I was continuing to recover in the ICU, I had a series of visions, two of which demonstrate the inextricable links between our personal trauma stories and those of all others.

The first vision I experienced took me into a forest of lush greenery and far away from metropolitan areas. There was no pollution in sight and the night sky shone a brilliant hue with every star beaming with vitality. It was as if the entire cosmos was showing off, celebrating the plentitude of life.

As I experienced the wonder and awe of nature's glory, a song began to rise from within me. I was surprised because I am not much of a singer, but I could not help but sing and dance in response to the beauty I was

Every Being Belongs

witnessing. Soon, I saw my partner and my children join me. I watched and heard them play instruments and sing songs I never heard before, songs they had never played before. We were singing, playing, and dancing together with a freedom that felt so utterly connected to the Whole of life.

It was not as though problems in our lives were erased; in fact, what made our singing and playing so powerful was our connectedness to the deep suffering within and around us, yet the realization that our lives were more than our suffering as well. Through our singing, the problems we faced were brought to transformation in light of the love that never abandons us.

Suddenly, we were out of the forest, as I witnessed the power of our music and celebration continuing, now beginning to touch the entire world, which opened to the healing flow. It was a powerful sight to see both the impact of that which is beyond logical explanation and also the sense that our personal lived experiences of suffering and celebration and love could invite others to their own transformation as well. I witnessed the power of lifting our voices together, allowing for our differences to deepen the sound, and I understood the ways in which our healing was not solely for our own benefit but was also meant to be offered to the entire world. It seemed as though the energy of wholeness was contagious and desired to be spread to all life.

In the next vision, I was taken on a journey to all corners of the entire world. I saw what seemed to be

Trauma and Renewal

every kind of geography, climate, habitat, and natural scenery. I intuited that all of it was interdependent and that my life and its suffering were intimately connected to others and the earth itself. While this experience moved me, it grew even more intense as I was taken to areas where many families and young children were living in tremendous poverty, lacking resources. The looks on their faces were ones of sadness, suffering, and trauma. It was as if the world had abandoned them, and they had little awareness of the preciousness of their own lives.

A feeling of deep despair and anger welled up within me. I thought, *How could it be that we live in such a sacred world, large enough to supply all our needs but so many are left without and treated as disposable?* It seemed as if the problems were too big and too insurmountable. And then at the moment I was overwhelmed by the weight, I looked toward the sky, and I saw what seemed to be clouds carrying an unlimited amount of material resources as though they were being poured out for these communities. I was surprised at how much was available, and I was happy to know that it would be granted to those most in need.

The experience seemed to call for a radical redistribution of resources where those most impacted by suffering would now be resourced and able to decide for themselves what they needed and how they would bring those resources to act in support of their community. It was a moment of profound empowerment. In witnessing

Every Being Belongs

this possibility, I felt something shift within me, which called me to continue to believe that there *is* a way forward. However, it was clear that the way forward requires our coming to consciousness of the immensity of suffering and requires that we also not turn away. The way forward requires resources and power to flow to those most impacted so that new worlds could be possible.

As I began to surface from these two intense visions, coming back into my present experience lying in the hospital, I felt the weight of the long road of recovery ahead of me. I then noticed many doubts arising within me, questioning what I just witnessed in the visions. I also felt sharp judgment toward those with money, power, and privilege whom I felt were responsible for the suffering, as those who had the capacity to change things but remained unwilling. I wondered what it would take for those in power to actually change.

As I felt some despair about the situation, my attention turned to watching the heart monitor next to my bed. It read 135 beats per minute, quite a fast heart rate for a person lying down. Likely the pain I was in mixed with the high intensity experience of the vision. As I looked at the heart monitor, I felt the divine communicating the constancy of love extended to me.

Although this was not a direct response to the thoughts and feelings that I was having, I realized I was being invited to anchor my own experience in the divine love that was being consistently extended to me

Trauma and Renewal

right where I was in the middle of my precarity. After a few moments of soaking in the truth that the sacred heart was pulsating for me, I then turned toward the window, seeing how outside rush-hour traffic clogged the roads. Hundreds of people were moving along the interstate. Each person pushing on to go to their next appointment or obligation or desired next place. Suddenly, I was filled with an overwhelming assurance that the divine heart was also beating for each one of them without discrimination. I felt consoled in knowing that life was held in this unfathomable love. I saw how divine mercy and care was continually being extended to them and the invitation was for each person to experience this and ground themselves very personally in this knowledge.

Yet once again questions arose. What about those I considered evil-doers, guilty of harming and hurting others but recalcitrant. I felt disturbed and wondered what love demands of them. So, I asked the divine, *Can your heart really beat for all people? Even those who have done the most harm?*

Before I could even pause to await a reply, I felt the resounding answer: A definitive and peaceful, yes. If love was truly love, then it has no limitations as to who is included. Then I realized the sacred heart was much greater than sentimentality or an obligation to forgive. In fact, there are no obligations with love, only a question offered unto us respecting our agency and personhood:

122

Every Being Belongs

What is it that you want? The sacred heart is not naive, not removed from the suffering, but rather is a courageous, even dangerous, and sacrificial reality that is continuously extending to all life in countless ways. I opened myself to this realization, allowing it to further integrate into my experience, and then I swiftly experienced a sense of freedom in knowing that I was loved in all my suffering and so was the rest of the world. I felt compelled to trust in the eternality of this love being offered to the Whole and to treat others in this sacred awareness.

What these visions taught me is that our healing is woven together.

While dominant cultures of society perpetuate exclusive treatments for people based on money, racial identity, or status, the divine love is extended to all of life. If we are to imagine forming new communities based in this truth, then we must build capacities for this love to grow wider and wider within us. Of course, learning to befriend all that we exclude is not just external work but is required of us internally as well. In fact, we find our greatest healing comes from learning to be present with the things inside that feel the most painful and are easy to push away. This is difficult work because it requires a death to our ego and our attachments to aspects of ourselves and of others who seem to mirror our preferred image of ourselves. But the time has come for us to be liberated from egocentric forms of connection and move

Trauma and Renewal

toward building new communities where love can flow to and from and through all beings.

Womanist theologian and founding pastor of the Fellowship of Affirming Ministries where we are members, Bishop Yvette Flunder, talks about the importance of building a radically inclusive community in which we "reach from the center to the farthest margin and back. When we reach for the ones who are the least accepted, we give a clear message of welcome to everyone. Jesus modeled this type of radical inclusivity when he openly received those most despised by society and the religious establishment."[3] For Flunder, this radical inclusivity begins with those the dominant cultures of society reject (including our more than human relatives) and with reimagining our lives so that we can live in great solidarity with one another.

But how do we relate to those who are doing harm and are unwilling to change? A radically inclusive community does not set boundaries for the community of human beings, though it's important to set and enforce limits in any relationships that are abusive or oppressive. Radical inclusion is not a relativism where anything goes, but rather a commitment to stop doing harm to ourselves, others, or the divine. And should a harm be perpetrated, we commit to a process of repair, doing our best to make amends.

Radical inclusion means we strive to live honest, grounded, and open lives that ultimately entrust all

Every Being Belongs

things to the care of the divine, as we withhold our judgments and continually turn inward, asking the divine for mercy and that we might be ever more transformed into love within our personal experience. We must continue to work tirelessly to invite love to do deep work within us, taking all the suffering we go through and inviting ever-new transformation so that we might co-create life anew together and in deep friendship.

Many of Jesus's parables featured radical belonging. A few notable examples of these include the search for lost sheep, the lost coin, and the prodigal son. However, one of the most powerful stories Jesus tells us about belonging is in the Gospel of Matthew where Jesus tells his followers to invite all people to a wedding feast. The text explicitly speaks of inviting all regardless of their background or moral character, turning upside down the cultural norms of preference to inviting your own group or those with privileged status. It is also important to notice that the telling of the wedding feast story comes right after Jesus turns over tables at the Temple, where he quotes the Hebrew scripture from Isaiah 56:7, "My house shall be called a house of prayer for all peoples," a challenge to the religious culture he grew up in for not being radically inclusive enough and greedily profiting off the poor. Jesus was angered that religion was used as a means of escaping or avoiding the actual suffering rather than being the means of comfort and transformation in tending to suffering with compassion.

Trauma and Renewal

Jesus also demonstrated an all-inclusive spirit the night before he was executed, during the last supper, where he offers his own life for the nourishment of his followers—even those who would betray him, deny him, and doubt his work in their lives. In fact, the only ritual Jesus created was this form of communion where he taught his followers to celebrate the generosity of life moving through him (and beyond him).

Life is granted to all freely. We can only receive it and give it back to reality for the sake of flourishing as well. I share this example not to encourage behavior that overlooks or diminishes the harm others do (in fact I recommend that for those traumatized by others, they take time and space away from those who caused hurt, in order to tend to their own healing), but I share it to demonstrate how we can approach trauma through a different lens that allows for a deeper work within us to emerge. It is this radically inclusive message and spiritual practice that Jesus asks his followers to teach to all people, so they might remember him. Jesus's example calls us to a life of faith with our suffering, to allow the compassion of life to guide us and prevent us from a sense of separation from the whole.

Our work toward a radically inclusive community must be a slow and careful process, not rushed or imposed but one in which we each walk gently with ourselves and others. As we do, may we be granted the divine mercy to experience this kind of reconnection to the wounded

Every Being Belongs

parts within ourselves, and then extend such care to others, whether friends and neighbors, those suffering in the world, and even to those blinded by violence. Once we feel a divine connection to them, we can begin to choose a radical act of love that includes truth-telling, setting boundaries, and even willingness to suffer (when necessary) so that liberative truth can be realized in small and big acts in relationship to the Whole.

SELF-LED SHARING

1. Ground your body in a way that is resonant for you. Pay attention to whether you feel spacious and open to sharing your experience with someone you deeply trust.

   a. If you notice you do not feel spacious or open but instead anxious or judgmental toward yourself, it's important to honor where you are and pause.

   b. If you continue to feel anxious, with little sense of spaciousness, see if you can engage a different practice that supports your feeling centered and at ease.

2. If there is still some reluctance to share your experience with another, see if you can become curious as to why (e.g., perhaps you are unsure if the person you are sharing with will judge you or perhaps you do not know where to begin and feel confused).

Trauma and Renewal

a. While there could be many reasons for reluctance to share, what is important is to really validate your own experience and hesitation in sharing.

3. Once you can identify those things preventing you from sharing, see if you feel comfortable just sharing those hesitations out loud with the person you hope will offer compassionate listening to you.

a. You can even ask them before you do with a statement like this: *I would really like to share my experience with you, but I am curious if you are open and available to hear some of the hesitation I am holding inside.* This is a good first step to sharing your own experience with one another, if they are not calm and grounded when you share your concerns about going deeper, then you, your body, will know that now is not the time and that finding another listening companion will be important.

4. If they confirm they are open to listening, you can let them know you are not looking for someone to give you answers or problem solve but to support you exploring your own experience more compassionately.

5. Again, you can ask them if they feel comfortable with your request. Extend compassion toward yourself, and remember that your story is only yours to tell, and you have full agency about how (your pace) and when (now or later) and with whom (in trust, which takes time to build) to share.

a. If you don't quite know where to begin, simply identify a word, feeling, thought, emotion, or sensation.

Every Being Belongs

6. After you share, take time to really validate your own concerns and express your hopes for what a time of sharing can mean.

    a. It can also be very powerful to ask the person listening to do the same as well, if they feel comfortable.

7. Inquire inside yourself if there is anything else that can be done to be more attentive to the needs of the "part" you shared.

8. Make a commitment to the part inside to be fully present and more compassionate to that part and notice how that changes your perspective on the experience you shared.

PART III

LIBERATIVE COMMUNITY

7

SEEING ONE ANOTHER

As we deepen our journey together, I'd like to investigate the theme of liberative community and its potential to support trauma transformation. Yet, it's important to first note that many communities *increase* harm for those who are suffering, especially religious and "spiritual" communities. And we must admit that not all traditional ways of practicing community are life-affirming. So, we proceed with awareness and intentionality. And no matter how sensitive and caring the community may be, there are ways to learn and grow in skills related to trauma care and trauma transformation.

In my training as both a spiritual care provider and psychospiritual practitioner, I have witnessed profound peer-to-peer as well as communal forms of healing. Both are necessary and helpful, and neither should be viewed as a replacement for the other. I've personally experienced both in times of my greatest vulnerability, as this chapter explores, and I also bring in reflections from my mother and father on their perspectives, seeing and acknowledging not only me, but themselves, together

Trauma and Renewal

with me in that vulnerable state. We'll then explore what it means for each of us to offer care and support to one another as together we navigate the treacherous road of trauma recovery.

To do that, I first want to invite you to reflect with me on three circles[1] of community that may be found attending to those in trauma. These are circles I experienced during and after my traumatic event: (1) strangers, (2) neighbors, and (3) family. These are circles familiar to others in their experiences after traumatic events, so you may find resonance recognizing these within your own journey. In this chapter I intentionally begin with the outermost circle (strangers) because it is a group we generally are least comfortable with. From there I then invite us to imagine how each of these circles can be re-created in our contemporary lives using a trauma-integrating spirituality to advocate for transformation in all our communities.

STRANGERS

As I reflect on all the care I received during and after my accident, my heart is overwhelmed. Many people came to my side and supported my journey of recovery, for which I am forever grateful. Some of the most important people in my own journey with trauma were strangers. These three people risked their lives to come to my aid when they found me lying in the middle of the freeway

Seeing One Another

left for dead after the accident threw me from my motor-cycle. As cars raced by at nearly eighty miles per hour, a young newlywed couple (about my age at the time) who recently emigrated from Egypt (I found this out later) were the first to stop and park their car in order to block incoming traffic to the lane I was lying in.

Aya[2] was the first person I noticed. I admit that I was surprised that anyone would be willing to stop and endanger themselves on the freeway for my sake (and of course many did not stop and kept driving by). Aya came to my side asking if there was anything she could do to alleviate the pain I was in. I didn't have an answer for her, but one thing I did ask her was if she could grab my phone and call my partner, so I could speak to her. It was an incredible gift to be able to hear my beloved's voice through Aya's care. Soon after, her husband, Mahmoud, approached me. And he also asked if he could help in any way. Just having their physical presence was huge for me in a moment when I felt incredibly alone. I asked him if he could help hold up my head, as I overextended it from the fall. For about ten minutes, he held my head gently, giving my sore neck some relief from the pain. While they were not trained care providers, they came to my side as strangers, moved by a deep compassion and even risked their own lives so that mine could be tended.

The third person to come to my side was another immigrant, from Lebanon, David. David was a motor-cyclist like me and told me he could not allow a fellow

Trauma and Renewal

biker to be left alone. While I do not believe he was medically trained, he found a rope from within his bag and somehow formed a tourniquet on my leg to attempt to stop the bleeding. The medics later informed me that the tourniquet sustained me in that life-threatening condition. It's hard to imagine my life being preserved without these three strangers. Each of them taught me so much that day about the power of seeing others in pain and moving toward the pain and need rather than running in the other direction.

It was not just that the strangers saw me on the side of the road. Others saw me, as I mentioned, but passed by. Yet these strangers were moved by a heart and spirit that sees the belovedness that dwells within each person. What these three strangers taught me is that there is a power in noticing others and their preciousness amid their vulnerability, even if you do not know or understand them. And when we act with that kind of seeing, lives can be literally saved.

My life was transformed and preserved by their seeing me as beloved that day. And their examples call me to greater courage, compassion, and faith, willing to go the extra mile for others.

Within the Christian tradition, there is a well-known story about this kind of deep witnessing known familiarly as the Good Samaritan. Jesus tells the parable in response to questions from religious leaders. They wanted Jesus to

Seeing One Another

define who our neighbor is, that is, who is worthy of our care. Though their question was meant to challenge him, Jesus's response radically subverted their assumptions.

Jesus tells them the story of several people from diverse backgrounds, each of whom noticed a person suffering near the road, but they avoided or ignored the suffering one. Yet one stranger from another land and culture traveling through was the sole person who stopped to show compassion for the one suffering who was considered "other" and was left for dead. The stranger passing through stopped, the one who truly saw the man who suffered as greater and more valuable than all else.

Jesus not only shares a model of the true neighbor, revealing that he is a representative from a community that the religious leaders who questioned Jesus were taught to despise, but Jesus shows how the truth of love is present in places and people we least expect. He demonstrates that all people can live this way by valuing others, even though we have been socialized into hierarchies that make certain bodies more valuable and worthy of our attention than others.

Our seeing, Jesus makes clear, leads us to a choice: either care for and engage others or harm others by avoiding their suffering. We are invited to become people who see others as beloved, which leads us to participate in the amelioration of suffering and the liberation of others. And in this participation, we realize our own belovedness, too.

Trauma and Renewal

In Jesus's life, he constantly engages suffering directly. And through his example we find a mature life is not one defined by identifying with a particular ethnic or religious group, but rather is defined by a person's capacity to see suffering and extend compassion. This kind of seeing is not a saviorism, an attempt to rescue all people from pain (which is a subtle form of pride). Instead, this seeing comes from a sense of deep solidarity, an awareness that we are all in this together.

While as a pastor I had taught this story many times, I never thought I would live through my own version of it. There I was, a Christian left for dead on the side of the road, when two Muslims and one Jewish person came to my aid in time of greatest need.

NEIGHBORS

In many religious institutions, there is an assumption that to love someone means to proselytize to them. This is not what love looks like. Love does not seek to create any monolithic or superior image. Some religious people can be exclusive and rigid. However, when it comes to transforming trauma, it's important that we move beyond insider–outsider paradigms and learn to honor one another, offering support where we can. This doesn't mean letting go of boundaries or practices of discernment for what life-affirming community looks like. Instead,

Seeing One Another

transforming trauma requires that we befriend those who are outside of our "group" (whether it be our religious or cultural group or the groups we have been socialized in) and live in relationships of care and mutuality.

In the five years prior to my accident, my partner and I had worked as event coordinators within an apartment community composed of people who were immigrants and predominantly low income. Our role was to provide weekly community gatherings for them, helping them to get to know one another. We enjoyed this work, getting out of our comfort zone, learning the customs and languages of others, and inviting them to feelings of connection and care.

North American society is quite individualistic, so intentionally creating our lives around community with others really challenged us but left a transformative effect. When news of my accident spread to those in our apartment community, we were shocked by the outpouring of love we received from them, who were our neighbors and now friends. Notes, gift cards, and food were given to us. And childcare offered. We were brought to tears by all those who began to show care and kindness toward us so freely. I remember one particular moment, when one of my neighbors came to visit me in the hospital and said, "You have done so much for our community, we want you to know that if you need anything at all, we will do it for your family as if they are our own." I was completely touched by the generosity and willingness to

Trauma and Renewal

support my partner and children, especially when I could not support them myself. We had built a radically diverse community with those who lived near to us, and it made all the difference in my recovery.

What would it look like for you, for me, to begin to more intentionally create neighborhoods of care? It looks like creating space and time to practice neighboring one another. It looks like having each other in our homes and taking the first step toward others rather than waiting for the "perfect opportunity." And it looks like treating one another with reverence and regard. This kind of neighbor care will not happen accidentally. It requires consistent devotion and attention. And when disaster or trauma hits, the community we have diligently built together can in turn diligently care for those who have nurtured community together. It changes everything.

As we reflect on the power of community and the care of neighbors, it can also be fruitful to make connections with how the early church understood community. The community of faith depicted in the book of Acts stood in contrast to the dominant culture of that time. This community shared with one another and held "everything in common." They shared food and material resources, and together were deeply devoted to a spiritual life modeled after Jesus's teachings. The community carried a contemplative spirit grounded in and lived out through material care and connection. That early

Seeing One Another

community was not perfect, but their example gives us a sense of how important it is to have communities ready to support us when trauma arises.

FAMILY

The last group in the circle of care that I want to mention is family. Family comes in all shapes and sizes and certainly goes beyond those who are biologically related to us, including "chosen family." Family simply consists of those relationships that provide us a sense of mutuality, affirmation, and deep care to companion us in the uncertainties that life affords. In my case, my biological family and my life partner are key. Their amazing resilience shone through the entire ordeal. Left to solo parent, my partner quickly arranged many logistical details of care for our children to visit me in the hospital as I recovered. She also kept daily life going for the children, ensuring they were able to have all their needs met. One year after the accident she decided to attend seminary to train as a spiritual director. She went to, as she said, "seek healing." I was and am in awe of her strength, perseverance, and courage.

My two siblings, Alyssa and Annalisa, both in stages of life transition, still did everything in their power to care for me in the hospital and to care for my children.

In the months after my time in the hospital, when I went to my parents' house to recover because it was more accessible, my siblings helped me shave, bathe. They cooked and helped transfer me from the chair to the bed because I literally could not do any of it on my own. This came at a great cost for them, and I am still blown away by their support. And as sometimes happens in situations of trauma with family, living through this experience together allowed me to connect to them in ways unknown to us before, as I was "the older brother." So, this allowed our roles to shift as we all learned new ways of relating to each other. I am forever grateful for the ways they showed up for me and my partner and the kids.

So many people came together, to partner and to do their share in the wake of my trauma. And I realize this is not the case for many people who suffer trauma. I hope my story shows how powerful it can be *when* it is available. And how critical it is to have many types of communities with us, whether loved ones, peers, and even "strangers" showing up for us to aid in our trauma care. Each and every being who offers any act of care to us along the way makes a world of difference.

ALMA'S REFLECTION

One of the most challenging moments as we accompanied Aizaiah involved the time he spent in the intensive care unit a few days after his sixteen-hour surgery. I recall perceiving how Aizaiah was experiencing God's touch through his own spiritual visions. He would often tell us, "I am healed, and

Seeing One Another

I can go home!" He indeed was being healed but not able to instantly walk like he wanted after a major surgery. I sometimes wondered how much impact the drugs had on his perceptions in that time. And I could feel the intense suffering he continued to go through.

What did not come as a surprise to me was that for all who entered his room, whether friends, nurses, doctors, or janitors, they would express a sense of sacred presence there. Aizaiah reminded each of us how much God loved us. He encouraged us to "look up" to God. I understood Aizaiah as bearing witness to heaven and earth as one. I also remember feeling that the nurses who cared for him were angels on earth helping families such as ours understand the healing process and the intense care and attention required. I experienced firsthand how vital and important care teams are in times of crisis.

In another specific moment, I recall Aizaiah's temperature was so high, he was restless. As a mother, I kept wondering how I could best offer him relief. I then found a hand fan and stood behind him. I started fanning him, praying for him, and telling him to rest. Aizaiah told me that seemed to help and asked me to keep fanning him because, as he said, he experienced in those moments the Shekinah glory of God.

I was a bit surprised and amazed, but it gave me the strength needed to fan him for over an hour. In that time, I wondered that I did not tire. In my heart, I knew that I would stand here as long as possible to fan him until he could sleep and feel some comfort. Perhaps the intensity of God's presence and healing was upon him and the fanning made it possible to continue the sacred healing. From these moments I learned we would all come through this fire refined.

AMOS'S REFLECTION

When Aizaiah needed a place to recover, we were lucky that our apartment had an available room downstairs with an accessible bathroom, more conducive to Aizaiah's recovery than his own family's apartment. His partner (and their two children) would drive up to visit daddy a few times each week while Aizaiah stayed with us after his release from the hospital. Our son's convalescence took up the entire downstairs of our home: A medically prescribed adjustable bed and mattress was brought into our living room, as well as two reclining sofas (all of which my wife generously secured for him).

The first few weeks of Aizaiah's time with us involved regular cleaning and tending to his wounds. Yes, a nurse would come two to three times a week, cleaning and bandaging his leg, and on the off days, I would support Alma in providing the needed care, on occasion taking the lead in care, when invited. Our daughter (who was almost three years younger than Aizaiah) was a godsend throughout. As Aizaiah would slowly begin to take steps toward healing himself, walking with assistance and showering with assistance, as he used the shower seat, his sister would assist her older brother. Often, both she and I would tag team

Seeing One Another

as Aizaiah sat in the shower, me bent over on my hands and knees to help with his lower extremities while she would assist variously with the upper body parts. Ours was a communal effort: his sister and I attending a bit more to the caring and cleaning, my wife, Alma (his mother), teaching up to two hundred students each day and then coming home to cook and otherwise relieve us.

The last time Aizaiah had been home for any length of time was almost a decade earlier, before he went off to college. From college he then was married and established his own family and home. This was therefore a renewal of sorts, but now under the posttraumatic stressful conditions of the horrendous accident and the multiple surgeries, he returned for a time with us. I think we did well for the three months it took for Aizaiah to regain the strength and mobility needed to return home, even with some back-and-forth times, as some of his initial efforts to get back to "normalcy" revealed he was not yet ready.

Yet it would be inaccurate to say what we lived through was only filled with ease and that we were always a nice happy family. Yes, there were more of these days than not; but occasional intense moments, no doubt related to accumulating stress amid the aftermath of the accident, challenged us all. One instance I recall involved my getting extremely angry and upset, so much so that I snapped at Aizaiah that no one was keeping him in our home against his wishes and that as things were unfolding, it would be better for him to move out and return to his family.

Trauma and Renewal

I do not now remember the exact details about why I lost my cool, although it had something to do with my perception of how he was treating his mother disrespectfully. Regardless—I am not trying to justify myself here—that this happened suggests that despite what is usually a wonderful relationship Alma and I have with our children and grandchildren, there are stresses after trauma. With the accident and all that unfolded in the aftermath, all of us met with heightened reactions (particularly me) that at other times of life are more diffused.

This incident also reminded me that my anger periodically surfaces. What "parts" of me do these outbursts of anger represent or derive from? My preliminarily formed Internal Family Systems understandings have been asking this more recently. As I reflect on the question, I see these bursts as connected to more childlike parts, which were formed in response to the sporadic anger I felt at the hands of my father (in his practice of "spare the rod, spoil the child," a modern paraphrase of a biblical proverb), something I have also observed in my siblings. Noting this is not about letting go of my responsibility but acknowledging where I have fallen short in losing patience and lashing out verbally to those around me, even to ones I love the most.

None of us are exempt from the trauma responses we have learned, even in caring families, but the first step is in acknowledging where we are and tending to those tender spots inside with enduring hope.

Seeing One Another

As my parents reflect, healing is not something done in isolation. Nor is it a one-time event. Trauma has ripple effects, and transformation must come through multiple networks of care. If one person endures trauma, it is likely that all those who love and gather around that person will also discover unresolved places longing for healing as well. Even in cases where we might be tempted to believe that we are "over it" or have "healed" that suffering, we find that in community together, there always seem to be new places that arise that call out for compassion and transformation. The work of wholeness is a lifelong journey.

All who offer care in the family or the community or in health-care systems know we have a long way to go before we can create adequate networks of care. For example, there continue to be large disparities for those who receive trauma support in the US. And within that US context, Asian and Asian Americans are among the highest of any racial groups who struggle to find culturally sensitive mental health care. Adding to the struggle to find care, Asian Americans rarely acknowledge their own need for care and are 50 percent less likely to receive mental health care than other racial groups[3] due to cultural stigma and a real fear of bringing shame to the family or their community if a diagnosis becomes public. Other racialized communities struggle to find mental health care support; as well, only 36 percent of Latinx adults who struggle with mental health ever access

Trauma and Renewal

care.[4] But silence around this issue does not mean it will go away. Silence can be deadly. An avoidance or minimization leads to hidden suffering that eventually leads to isolation, anxiety, and intensifies the mental health challenges of origin. We long for and need communities that can support us throughout our journeys—and those facing trauma often require not only the support for physical healing but the often longer-term effects of trauma that, when "ignored," lead to issues around mental health.

Here again is why culturally informed liberative communities are necessary for those who endure trauma as well as for those providing care for the traumatized. Trauma companions rarely have safe spaces to share their experiences around traumatic events. And for those who are members of a marginalized social group, this is even rarer. Many believe the person who was traumatized firsthand is the one who "had it worst," so caregivers therefore minimize their own experience, and this neglect halts their own healing journey. It is vital we normalize the struggles that accompany this work so that all in the trauma community take time to reflect, seek support, and nurture patience in the long journey of healing.

When we talk about communities important to trauma transformation, we know not all of us have the benefit of communities that support us when trauma hits. As noted earlier, sometimes it is our very family or community that is the source of trauma. Therefore, this

Seeing One Another

discussion around community is not focused so much around any one form of community (although we ought to give our best to cultivating loving connection where we can) but about rethinking our capacities to contribute to trauma-transforming communities and also remaining open to the various forms of community that are available to us—whether a plant, an animal, or the stories of those who have come before us who were "alone," too, and so strengthen us in our journeys of trauma transformation so that we know that we are not the first or the last to experience certain dimensions of solitude.

Those of us who care about building these communities have the aim of seeing more clearly, effectively, and compassionately. We also expect that in any community, there will be conflict and tension. There is vast diversity in community, and that is partially what also makes it so powerful. We all bring different needs, ideas, experiences, resources, and hopes to the table, and we must work together to work them out. Of course, all these dynamics are intensified through the presence of trauma. But as we looked at previously, there are also many skills we can develop when relating to one another as traumatic situations arise.

For those who are Christ followers, we live in the aftermath of the cross and its traumas. Many are quick to focus on the resurrection but also forget that the resurrected Christ left his community just forty days after the resurrection, a loss after a loss. They forget Jesus's most

Trauma and Renewal

emphatic advice was to love one another. Jesus's loved ones still had to learn how to manage life without him, but their primary task was to build liberative communities together. And in many ways that is why the practice of communion is important. It is one way of reencountering the life of Christ (birth, death, and resurrection) in a context of community, even after Jesus had left them.

As I think about the early church and the liberative community just being formed, growing at a rapid rate, I imagine how much trauma must have continually surfaced for them. As new people were added to the community, they were told about the life, death, and resurrection of Jesus. Their personal wounds must have arisen as they shared a community trauma and aftermath. For them, the resurrection would have no meaning, if it were not for the trauma and death Jesus endured. And neither would new life in Christ be comprehensible without deeply touching the traumatized places inside.

No wonder the early church was a messy and difficult community to be in! However, one thing was certain; they were not a community that would do business as usual. They would commit to welcoming others into the community to be materially cared for and spiritually supported to undergo the long road of healing. They made a commitment to each other to not overlook the suffering, to be a place where it was acknowledged and worked with.

Seeing One Another

For our communities today, what would it mean to follow this model? To invite the realities of trauma among us? And what would it look like to bring our spiritualities that are life-affirming into the mix? It would certainly require bringing a different sort of honesty to our situations and a willingness to keep engaging the trauma with one foot in solidarity with suffering and one foot grounded in the love that surrounds and fills all through and through.

We cannot walk this journey alone; we need others to support us through the highs and lows.

Long after I was out of the hospital, my body was still metabolizing the suffering, even as my injury was physically apparent for the six months afterward, as I learned anew to walk, albeit with a limp. Now I continue to walk with that limp and the after-effects of my injury, some of it more physical in nature and some of it internal and invisible to the eye but apparent to my heart. Even still I continue to be aware of how this event invited me to deeper reflection and holistic healing—a healing not only for me, but my entire community, even the entire world. To truly hold this awareness takes a lifetime of learning, but we can and must absolutely grow in our capacities for awareness, healing, and growth together.

Trauma and Renewal

A PRACTICE OF DEEP SEEING

1. Find a place in nature (whether physical or virtual), which you experience as grounding or restorative.
2. Allow yourself a few moments to simply take in the space you are in relation to.
3. Notice any aspect of this place that seems to stand out. Perhaps it is a tree, a flower, a rock, a living animal, or a rock shining under the water. The more focused you can be on one small aspect, the better.
4. Extend curiosity toward that aspect on which you've set your gaze.
5. Notice how it interacts and relates with the environment around it.
6. Invite that aspect, which you are in relation with, to share with you any gift or offering of nourishment.
7. Breathe in the gift to your body and feel that chosen aspect in its relational gifting presence within you.
8. Honor that gift now by considering one thing you might do to deepen your awareness and experience of this insight throughout your day.
9. Share your experience with one or more trusted people, if you are comfortable doing so, telling them about this gift or what came up for you in this time.

8

EXPANDING COMPANIONSHIP

I preached my first sermon at the age of seventeen and became a licensed minister in a local congregation at the age of nineteen. With the zeal of new convert and a naive idealism, I assumed the "good news" could fix all the problems of the world if people simply believed. One day, though, a teenager came to me asking, "If God's promises are so real, why is there so much loss and grief in this life?"

I was floored by the question. I had no answers, no solutions, and as a minister, nothing comforting to offer. In subsequent years of ministry, I've learned there is often no ultimate answer that can fully satisfy us. I've also learned that people are not looking for ultimate answers, but rather for someone to simply walk with them in those questions that cannot be answered.

After the series of visions in the hospital, there were multiple moments during the first week of recovery that I felt completely healed, as though I could walk out of the hospital. My body told a different story, however, likely due to a mixture of the drugs I was given for pain

Trauma and Renewal

along with the excitement around the visions I witnessed. Responding to my claims of healing, there were multiple instances where my family and/or the medical staff would tell me, "Yes, God is with you, and you are healed, *but now* is the time to rest."

Like many facing trauma, I wanted to rush healing. In retrospect, this makes sense. Raised in an immigrant household of the global majority and in churches that proclaimed victory but rarely talked about grief or trauma aloud, we never made space to hold the suffering. Churches taught us to pray and trust in God's goodness, but like that teenager who confronted me with clarity noted, the problem was that many times life *is not* full of goodness.

As people who struggled under the weight of sexism, poverty, racism, ableism, and classism, we know this, but we never allowed ourselves to name it, for fear that we would drown in the overwhelming truth of it. But when we refuse to name the fullness of our experiences, they do not simply go away with time and transform themselves. We must learn to work with our lives as they are, knowing deep down we are loved right here and right now, in the middle of whatever arises. This is not just a matter of "believing harder" or having more faith but about learning new skills that can assist us in living honestly, naming the truth of our lives.

When I reflect upon all the people and systems that worked together for my care, the list seems endless: first

Expanding Companionship

responders, strangers on the highways, friends, hospitals, doctors, neighbors, surgeons, physical therapists, social workers, chaplains, occupational therapists, spiritual teachers and leaders, psychologists, and many more. And because trauma care is not a one-size-fits-all approach, many are required in the work toward holistic transformation. We need diverse tools, ideas, approaches, and skill sets to tend to our whole person.

Within the context of trauma, those of us committed to liberative community must be conscious and aware of especially these two dynamics: (1) the need to destigmatize our ideas about suffering and (2) the need for a renewed imagination around what trauma transformation can entail, including the embrace of multiple (and sometimes contradicting) cultural and spiritual models and methods.

In the churches of my upbringing, suffering was responded to in mainly two ways. The first, was to explain that suffering is the result of some error the person (or an ancestor) made and that the person was now experiencing this suffering as punishment or some greater "lesson" being taught about the spiritual life. The second was that the devil or some evil spirit was behind the pain we were feeling. Especially for those who grew up in conservative faith traditions, those asking spiritual questions around trauma may have been tempted to hold similar beliefs. And while there may be occasions to be

155

Trauma and Renewal

sympathetic to aspects of this thinking, the reality is that neither of the above explanations bear much fruit when it comes to the actual suffering we endure. And unfortunately, faith communities often end up demonizing the person while dehumanizing the holistic experience.

There are many times in life that suffering is not the consequence of any prior action committed. Take, for example, those who endure systemic oppression of all kinds. Or take the case where suffering is intentionally undergone because of love of others. We can see the latter in the civil rights movement, founded on the practice and teachings of Christian nonviolence. One of the key core principles of nonviolent social change involves the willingness to suffer (when necessary) and do so alongside those who are struggling against injustice so that new visions of justice could be possible. To be clear, the call to willingly suffer, if necessary, does not advocate *for* suffering or imply that suffering should ever be desired. In fact, Jesus's prayer requesting the "cup pass" from him was a clear sign that whenever possible, we should seek to avoid suffering. However, in cases when communion with those who are hurting or marginalized, including interior dimensions in communion with our own personal experience, may be present, they can lead us to testify to a solidarity of love and renewal.

There is never a "greater purpose" to suffering; it just is. However, *how* we engage the reality of suffering can

Expanding Companionship

make all the difference. Our conviction with suffering, however, is that we are loved and called to pursue holistic flourishing in every possible way. Voluntary suffering is that which flows from deep love for all life and as such does not appease the status quo but directly challenges it, revealing oppression for what it is and the possibility that our lives can embody that which is beyond oppression. It is a conscious choice to partner with the divine in life, as we affirm ways that new potentials can emerge.

Interestingly, in many spiritual traditions, voluntary suffering has long been a place where many have encountered the divine. Think of the ascetic traditions, which are not seen as socially acceptable in our times, and, of course, have many problematic aspects that must be addressed. However, there is no doubt that there are stories of willful abstinence that have brought benefit to the human experience and broken us open to a greater love. One such example is Julian of Norwich, who described the crucifixion of Christ as a call to cosmic solidarity with the whole of creation.[1] Through these examples, we see we must destigmatize our ideas about suffering: never to romanticize it, but to build capacities to work with it in community so all are led to a greater plentitude of life rather than to despair, self-hatred, or harsh judgment.

It is imperative we find creative ways to rethink how suffering is experienced in our lives and find expansive ways to be life-affirming toward the suffering so that it

Trauma and Renewal

might be transformed through our lives. The reality is we need to become more aware of the plethora of healing capacities available to us, and do what we can to hold space for ourselves and others, moving with focus and open-hearted responsiveness.

While there are many benefits that arise from the myriad ways dominant cultures have concentrated on the importance of mental health, well-being, and thriving, there is also a great danger in pathologizing experiences that are not considered pleasant or enjoyable. This certainly occurs within many trauma models where people in pain can easily be seen as problems that need to be fixed rather than human beings in need of more skillful and compassionate support.

And the problem worsens for those interested in spiritually integrative trauma transformation, where their interest is decried by religious leaders who denounce insights from the social sciences as they instruct adherents to simply pray things away. In many cases, the spiritual prescriptions by these religious leaders do not "work," leaving the person who is suffering to feel as though something is inherently wrong with them, their prayer, their faith. The combination of toxic theology, cultural and legacy oppression combined with a lack of understanding and holistic training are deadly. The result is significant unintentional harm brought by religious leaders unaware of how trauma works and the long-lasting effects it has.

Expanding Companionship

The challenges are heightened in the shadow of a medical system that historically has been weaponized against marginalized communities (including blaming those who are oppressed for the suffering and attempting to "fix" or heal people rather than join them on their journey). We witness how many communities are left without culturally affirming options for trauma support, who then are blamed for their ongoing struggles. We clearly need new paradigms of spiritually integrative trauma companionship.

Yet we understand that no one person, culture, spiritual orientation, practice, or model will suffice for our collective liberation. We must overcome our monocultural mind, which only identifies wholeness and healing in accordance with dominant narratives and the status quo. But we need each other and require many different healing modalities for trauma transformation.

We cannot assume that each person's needs are the same, so we need intentionality around access to care if we are to be committed to trauma-integrating liberative communities. We know many people face barriers when it comes to receiving trauma support. Perhaps the most significant barrier is financial resources, followed by cultural stigma around trauma and mental health. Many communities of color, for example, experience many cultural obstacles to trauma support, including language barriers, the many forms and paperwork processes required in health care that are

Trauma and Renewal

foreign to them, and a lack of knowledge about how to obtain support and where it's available. As if that is not daunting enough, for those who may seek out trauma support, the many paradigms of mental health care that are overindividualized do not align with the collectivist instincts inherent in cultures of the global majority. One example of how this difference plays out is in the acknowledgment around individuation and collective healing. For Confucian cultures, the collective is very important. While Eurocentric mental health practitioners might simply tell someone to leave a toxic relationship and focus on the individual's happiness, for those coming from different backgrounds, it is not that easy or culturally applicable for those whose background is grounded in the consideration of others.

Currently, there is a significant lack of culturally sensitive mental health professionals skilled in ways of being and healing that can validate and learn from the cultural values of those from the global majority. Thankfully, there are new programs and a diversity of trauma partners emerging that consider how mental health care can be offered in culturally sensitive ways. There is a stark need for more education, resourcing, and sharing of power both inside mental health professions but also in our communities. And while getting professional help is certainly important and recommended, there are many skills lay people can learn that can be extended to each other in everyday community.

160

Expanding Companionship

One of the first skills we can learn is to practice nonjudgment. So often, our first instinct in relating to others is judgment. We deem something "good" or "bad." And while there may be some value in using categories so our minds can process information, often this unconscious habit creates barriers to connecting with those who are suffering. To begin practicing nonjudgment, we might simply notice the judgments that arise, recognizing that those judgments likely carry some important information about our own personal history that is worth reflecting on at another time. We can also check in with ourselves, asking ourselves if we are accessing enough curiosity to truly stay open and interested in the person who is sharing the story. Often for those who suffer, the greatest pain is feeling alone and having no one to affirm the struggle we experience. Those who practice nonjudgmental awareness can affirm the experience of others for what it is, which is a vital aspect of intimate belonging. Rather than becoming prescriptive with pain, we can take a moment to practice nonjudgmental awareness as we meet with and affirm others and their experience.

Another important skill we can learn in supporting others in their suffering is related to nonjudgment but involves supporting the agency of others, that is, the practice of seeking consent. So often the things we suffer from have happened due to circumstances beyond our control—which is the case for those in trauma response. An important aspect of healing for trauma survivors is

Trauma and Renewal

regaining agency around their bodies, including their rights, needs, and desires. Consent requires that those supporting people in trauma provide multiple options. This is crucial especially in collectivist communities where some may feel obligated to do what others are doing or to have a particular response to trauma, or to play a particular role in the family or household. To know they have options and a choice can be liberating for people as they make decisions, knowing they continue to be loved and honored. So, for those of us committed to liberative communities, giving people space to opt in or opt out of conversations, experiences, or any predetermined expectations can be significant in transforming patterns of trauma.

Even in cases where we feel we have something helpful to offer, it is a good practice to check in with the other person and see how they feel about our offering some insight before we share it. As a researcher and learner by nature, I love offering connections to new ideas that may be helpful to others, but I have had to work hard at unlearning some of those tendencies, by first asking myself, *What is it that people are looking for? Can I start with where the person is, not just where I am or want them to be? And once I have a sense for where the person is, might there be others who are a better fit to support them at this time?* It is crucial we learn to identify where people are and what they are looking for first as a starting point toward true care and connection.

Expanding Companionship

Last, for those of us seeking to support individuals affected by trauma, we need a renewed imagination for understanding all the different forms that trauma transformation takes. As it relates to cultural and spiritual models, we know that many trauma care practices are inherited from Eurocentric cultures. And while that does not mean that these practices don't offer something beneficial as different from what may be currently most utilized in a person's cultural setting, for those who are immigrants (or have parents who are) or of non-European descent, the Eurocentric models may be missing relevant aspects for transformation, and may benefit from learning from and updating practices related to a more diverse array of people, communities, needs, and resources.

One insight I've appreciated in my own community as a child of immigrants comes from Confucian and Mexican cultures, which include deep reverence and awareness of ancestors. In Confucian understanding, there is a keener sense of how the ancestors impact us today and how we might partner with them for wholeness. In Mexican American cultures, Dia de Los Muertos is another important day of remembrance for all the gifts our ancestors have offered to us. While ancestor reverence has been demonized by colonial forms[2] of Christianity, that has also meant cutting off an essential healing ingredient for people of color. And not only people of East Asian or Mexican descent—there are

Trauma and Renewal

plenty of people and cultures who connect to ancestral teachings and practices, including African and Indigenous peoples around the world.

Some Eurocentric trauma professionals are barely beginning to talk about the importance of ancestral healing, even as many cultures of the global majority have long-established practices for communing with the ancestors, paying respects, and contributing to the healing of their family. Ancestral practices can have powerful effects (positive and negative) when it comes to trauma, and trauma companions would do well to learn from traditions that have long recognized ancestral dimensions related to our suffering. There are significant reasons why and examples of how those coming from cultures of the global majority may struggle with anti-oppressive ways of doing trauma care, even as there are also aspects of those same cultures and practices that can guide us toward a more liberative and culturally informed practice of care.

Another gift from collective cultures related to healing is the recognition that our life experiences do not just belong to us as individuals, but rather are relational experiences, which tie us to our communities. Trauma is often talked about in very individualistic ways, and while it's true each experience is individuated, there remain bridges and connecting points to pay attention to. And Confucian and Indigenous cultures can offer us guidance and practices as we think about trauma in a context of

Expanding Companionship

community. Trauma impacts the ways we show up in the public square, from our family systems to our loved ones and our friends, but it also impacts how we relate to the most vulnerable in society.

From a relational point of view, trauma transformation can lead us to greater care and compassion for all who suffer in the world. And, yes, understanding trauma as relational presents both promises and problems. Important questions arise such as, *What would it look like to be truly supported in our trauma transformation work by those outside of our culture, language, and tradition? What are ways we can learn to avoid rushing to provide answers or "fixes," but instead simply walk with others in the terrifying and glorious experience of being alive as we create space in our lives and encourage that space in others to sit with the experiences as they arise?*

In building supportive liberative communities, a final key to imagining trauma transformation requires humility. The presence of humility invites us to recognize that we are all human beings in the making and that perfection is not the absence of mistakes, but rather an ongoing way of learning to relate to our mistakes with compassion. We are ever on the way to realizing the precious and sacred gift of life, and we are in this discovery together. In fact, we need each other to help us fully realize this gift.

At times humility calls us toward practices of repair when intentional or unintentional harm has been committed (profound examples of this intentional repair

Trauma and Renewal

can be found in the practice of restorative justice, for example, or in courageous communication), and other times it calls us to prioritize ongoing learning and development. Our collective liberation is not realized through one path but through many, and it is ever new.

We begin this work by embracing our own embodied experiences, in all their joys, complexities, and awkwardness. Being alive is something altogether uniquely wondrous, bizarre, and a gift to cherish. We learn to live this embrace best when we are intentional about community life and relationships that integrate our holistic experiences and that are spiritually supportive, acting out our collective liberation one step and one grace at a time.

A PRACTICE OF CULTURAL RESOURCING

1. Consider a few of the healing practices in your own upbringing, culture, or tradition. You may want to write those down, to reflect on them.
2. What were you told about those practices? Were they viewed positively? Negatively?
3. Have you experienced any of those healing practices yourself? What was that like?
   a. If not, is it possible to inquire or become curious about healing practices from your cultural heritage you were not exposed to, perhaps even visit places or communities that support those healing practices?

Expanding Companionship

   b. If you have experienced those healing practices, what would it be like to return to those practices and engage them again?

4. Could you consider ways to creatively integrate those practices into your daily life?

9

RISING AGAIN ... AND AGAIN

If we are lucky to live through and transform traumatic experiences, we may feel called to support others in transforming theirs. And doing that work requires participating in liberative community, where multiple members work side by side to offer sustenance at various points in the healing process. The etymology of the word *sustain* shows us that being sustained consists of being held (*tenere*) from below (*sub*). Being held from below means that our entire existence is being cared for and is being addressed holistically. Unfortunately, we very rarely sense that our entire being is being held up and regarded. One of the challenges we face around this comes from the dominant mind-set that gave rise to the modern sciences, a mind-set obsessed with classifying, differentiating, and breaking down our experiences to their tiniest fractions. This obsession with classification and fragmenting into smaller parts, means that we tend not to see the whole of ourselves, but rather sections or splinters at any given time. The result is that aspects of ourselves feel held and understood but other parts of us feel demonized, exiled, and unworthy of our attention.

Rising Again ... and Again

Unfortunately, the fragmentation continues in the psychological sciences, where we tend to think of well-being in single domains at a time rather than holistically (Internal Family Systems therapy stands out as an exception here). Take, for example, how some think about social well-being as paramount, others insist mental well-being is critical, pastors make a case for spiritual well-being, and trainers spur on physical well-being, and so on and so forth. And while these categories have a place, each is monoperspectival and narrow in and of itself. To move to a holistic way of relating requires a different way of knowing and interacting with life that transcends and integrates (rather than excludes) our bodies and minds. Indeed, it is the work of spirituality that coheres the parts, that helps us move toward a holistic renaissance.

While my intention is not to wage war against the sciences (they absolutely have an important place in our thriving), I am calling us to see more holistically rather than in the limitations of categorized differentiations. As a community, I want to invite us all to tell new stories that feature the multiple aspects of ourselves and not reduce ourselves to any one dimension (such as our social identity, our profession, our religious or cultural orientation). Because anything we neglect, which longs for connection, will only come back to haunt us and continue splintering us. The good news is that we do not need look far to discover the many other models that can help us relate more holistically.

Trauma and Renewal

INTERCULTURALITY AND WHOLENESS

One way forward is to begin with an intercultural approach. If we are going to be free from what I call "the bondage of fragmentation," where aspects of our lives must be ignored, dismissed, or rejected for us to "belong," the antidote is to develop an intercultural paradigm where many things can coexist simultaneously. An intercultural and relational understanding of life means that there are many important dimensions to our lives, and no one aspect is considered greater than another. For trauma to be transformed we must embrace the whole of our lives and communities to experience wholeness.

Interculturally speaking, we have so much to learn from those who are different from us because no one tradition has all the answers to the questions we ask. We need each other. From this intentionality around cultural difference, we can learn that it is okay for things to not always arrive at perfect harmony, to remain uncertain. If we can do that, we begin to see a plethora of open-ended possibilities always unfolding and arising across our lives. Regardless of what we have been through and where we are today, the story is not over. Because it is constantly unfolding, we can learn to begin again.

Many spiritual and cultural traditions of the global majority affirm this intuition of the holistic as unitive and unfolding. Again, my aim is not to advocate for any one tradition, but to highlight that being alive in this wonder-

Rising Again ... and Again

fully diverse world means working with the diverging, ebbing and flowing realities we encounter. The call is to embrace the journey one step at a time, learning to make space within our shared lives for these moving dynamics and extending grace to this lifelong process (a process that according to many traditions perhaps continues past death). Let us consider then how our spiritual communities can be places of holistic well-being, providing nourishment with foods and material resources, practicing rhythms of rest and work that offer ongoing renewal, and guiding each other toward spiritual practices that help to ground and center us or give us hope even amidst the terrors of trauma and trauma recovery.

AMOS'S REFLECTION

Having done work on disability theology long before Aizaiah had his accident, I had been attuned to the theoretical aspects of injury and impairment. Accompanying our son over the last few years has put palpable flesh—pun intended, considering the grafting of flesh from his thigh to cover the hole in his leg!—on the theoretical bone. Jacob's limp, or Zaccheus's perpetual short-staturedness, or the scarred wounds in Jesus's hands and feet and the hole in the side of his resurrected body—these biblical images of the marks of impairment have become personal in and through our son's experiences. The physical wound can heal in this or that respect, but it becomes a mark on our bodies and, in light of

Trauma and Renewal

our experience, a sign of who we—our immediate family in this case—have been and are becoming.

In my case, the secondary trauma I lived through foregrounded afresh unresolved trauma that I have not been as attentive toward. Not only did that show up in my reactive inclinations but in my own sense of unresolved pain, fears, and anxieties. When I was seven or eight, I waited for hours before my father, who usually came to pick me up from school, remembered me and arrived; how has that led to my own worries of abandonment? When I was eleven, not long after our family emigrated from Malaysia to California, the accumulated stresses led to a breakdown of relationship between my parents and persisted for a week or two; how has that shaped the husband and father "parts" of who I am today, for good or ill? When I was twelve or thirteen, I was taunted as one "fresh off the boat" on my school bus by a white kid; how might such traumatization have contributed to an internalized "perpetual foreigner" identity that has in turn driven my "successes" as a theologian?

Yet if we live on this side of history, what theologians call the "eschaton," then ours is inevitably a sojourn into the depths of Holy Saturday. Jesus's own Holy Saturday journey was a descent into the depths of hell, to accompany and then release the prisoners, as the biblical tradition intimates. So also, our calling is to accompany one another into the depths of our traumas, not to enact any once-for-all deliverance (impossible on this side of history) but to ameliorate its debil- itating effects, over and over, since fresh traumatic disruptions are always on the horizon. However, if we lock arms with

Rising Again ... and Again

each other, this is already central to the reconnection so vital for trauma survival; and if we persist in this connectivity, then the narrative of traumatization is already being renewed, not in the pain suffered by oneself but as borne together in each other's company. I, in other words, continue the journey with my son not only for his own sake but also for mine, and for each of us who are part of this family.

My father's reflections point to building liberative communities of sustenance, not as a one-time affair, but through constant and continuous attention. Additionally, it's important to note that building communities of sustenance is also not about our communal power to prevent the worst from happening but knowing there will be moments when tragedy hits and that we respond in community, interculturally. Jesus taught those who were oppressed and suffering not to worry because each day has enough to be concerned with and there would be provision ultimately coming from the divine through people and places we least expect. As I understand this teaching, we are to practice our deepest commitments today—in the here and now, trusting that as we do, love continues the work through us and serves as course correction each step of the path.

Rather than living for outcomes or being attached to the way we want things, practicing compassion toward life as we are experiencing it today opens us to life as an ever new and emerging adventure. Practicing sustenance means holding one another from below today so that

Trauma and Renewal

our hearts and minds stay clear and open, ready for the unexpected that may come. This doesn't mean becoming worst-case scenario ultraplanners and attempting to rid ourselves of all uncertainties (which is indeed the technocratic mind-set that already threatens the earth). On the contrary, this practice requires that we develop the spiritual capacities of sustaining in community with one another the earth and the divine. And sustaining practices remind us that there are other actors beyond the human realm with whom we share this life and who affect our experience.

It is in the never-ending potential for transformation that I find the resurrection promise of Christ so poignant. We are called to rise again. A rising that is not a once and done for all time but a continual arising, recognizing the gift in each moment and in each breath. This is a call to the Whole, to all interdependent life. Many understand Christ's resurrection to be the overcoming of death and suffering, but I invite us together to consider how this promise is not one that claims life will hold no more suffering, but rather that our suffering takes on an entirely different character in the light of an ever-arising resurrection. Contemplate the butterfly with me for a moment, long looked to as a symbol of the resurrection: The butterfly can only be what it is through the caterpillar, which has a very different and unique form. The butterfly is in no way better than the caterpillar, nor is the caterpillar superior to the butterfly. Both the caterpillar and the butterfly must relinquish form so

Rising Again ... and Again

that the next version of life may emerge. How can we say the butterfly is a better creature when it too shall pass? Perhaps the miracle of life is that nothing comes by accident, but only as life continues to make a way where no way seemed possible at all.

Liberative community can be strengthened through our trust in the promise of this kind of resurrection—a promise of suffering that is engaged and brought into a love that continually transforms all things where wholeness is not a destination but an experience of communion. Perhaps this is why the early church was a profound place of trauma transformation and why the church's community was described as increasing in numbers daily, as many were attracted to this community. Their attraction was not because they had all the answers but because they honestly asked and lived the questions. The early church was full of suffering, yet it was a gathering of people that engaged it through love, committed to holistic vitality for all people, beginning with the oppressed.

Of course, an orientation and posture of resurrection in community does not preclude practicing discernment or suggest that everything goes. Rather, it seeks to be continually conscious of the gamut of experiences we all live through, and learns to engage that breadth. An orientation of resurrection, while it may be personal, requires the presence of others who can help us and offer us care, insight, and imagination when things are indeed bigger than an individual can move through alone.

Trauma and Renewal

In that spirit of freedom, I conclude with a poem I wrote after my accident, "Today is the day." It can also easily be sung:

> *Today is the day, a day to be free.*
> *Today is the day, for you and for me.*
> *Today is the day, where all shall sing.*
> *Today is the day, we will all be free.*
> *We will all be free.*

May we learn to walk with another through the valleys, the mountains, the rivers and oceans, through the fires, and storms, and all that we see and all that we do not, bearing witness to a liberation available to all, inviting us to return home to ourselves and to a life of transformation and joy.

CREATING AN INVENTORY OF RESILIENCE PRACTICES

1. What are spiritual, mental, communal, and embodied practices you can enact today that will benefit you and your community tomorrow, even if we cannot predict what tomorrow will bring?
2. Make a list of the various ways that we can even now begin to build important and needed capacities pertinent to meeting crisis. These might include things such as truth-telling, listening, apologizing, and finding grounding when things become too intense.

AFTERWORD

Wholeness Is Not a One-Time Event

Writing this book and communicating the vastness of both suffering and the accompanying spiritual visions granted to me in the aftermath of trauma has been a daunting task. At various moments throughout the writing process, when I noticed myself avoiding certain dynamics in my experience, I needed to work them out in therapy, spiritual direction, and with other trusted people before finally writing them for the wider public.

At points I questioned if I was doing the right thing by sharing this material in a narrative. Adding to the challenges, this book was written intergenerationally, as both my mother and my father were willing to contribute to the wider story by writing honestly about their lived experiences working with secondary trauma. As a person of color, like my parents, I know we rarely have the space or support to discuss such events intergenerationally (nor sometimes is this even possible or desirable), but I hope that this offering can begin to open new paths of wholeness across generations in our racially (or otherly) minoritized communities. I am also grateful for the

Trauma and Renewal

many people I met from all walks of life who graciously listened to some of my story as I was writing this book, affirming the wisdom it contains, and encouraging me to keep writing.

As I was stumbling my way through the writing process, I was reminded of all the times I had fallen after my accident. There have been at least three separate occasions where I have slipped, lost balance, and reopened the wounds from my accident causing me to go to the emergency room for a new round of stitches. Each time I have fallen, I faced the same sorts of intense feelings and questions and consolations and support that were present in my initial trauma. And each time I was also reminded to return to the love that has carried me through and through. In each fall, I have learned that the process of transformation does not ultimately depend upon my will, nor does it happen according to my timelines. And though it does not seem so at first, this is good news because the strength of our lives is not found in an ability to surpass what is difficult but in our willingness to begin again, strengthening the Whole, as we walk one another back home.

At various moments of writing this book, I felt a profound and sacred connection. I consciously included the wisdom of ancestors and spiritual leaders (both alive and passed) in the process and understood this book to be truly a "team effort." And as the writing of this book ended, I realized this process was also a profoundly

Afterword

healing and integrative process allowing me to go deeper into my own path of transformation.

My intention with this book was simply to return to the depths of my experience and to share it as honestly and clearly as possible, without rushing to any final conclusions, because I do not have any ultimate answers or recommendations. However, I do believe love is at the heart of it all, and if this book invites only one other person to a greater expansiveness, it will be worth it. And I look forward to hearing how love finds its way into new areas of our lives and how it will be freshly revealed and reimagined for those who read this book and share their stories with others.

My prayer for you is that your journey be filled with the glory and hope of the resurrection, today and evermore. May we continue to taste and celebrate together the fullness of this profound life we share.

ACKNOWLEDGMENTS

There were so many wonderful people who contributed to the writing of this book.

I first have to say thank you to my family. Neddy, Serenity, Valor, Rio, and Kairo: You are the most treasured people in my life, and I am so grateful to God for bringing our family together. Each of you is so beautiful, kind, and encouraging. Thank you for being my greatest teachers about love day in and day out. I recognize the patience, grace, and the sacrifices you have made to allow me time for writing and study. I pray that your gift to me will be fruitful in the world's healing. I pray for each of you that you discover the sacred welling up in the middle of your days, and that each moment would be filled with a sense of aliveness and joy. I pledge my support to do all that I can so you can live out your divine vocation, too.

I am amazed by the courage and humility of my parents, Alma and Amos, who played an instrumental role in making this book a reality. I was unwilling to write it alone and I am grateful they were open to my persistence of doing this *en conjunto* and saying "yes" to the invitation to cowrite about some of the most difficult moments we have faced. I know it is no small task to go into deep trauma healing work, let alone to share any of

Acknowledgments

it publicly. I honor you both for who you are, who you have been to me, and who you are becoming. I know our ancestors are smiling down on us.

I acknowledge the wisdom and genius of my editor, Lil Copan. I am honored to publish with Orbis again for their world-renowned reputation at the intersections of mysticism, spirituality, and liberation theology. Lil, your candid feedback, advocacy for my work, and personal care throughout the entire publication process has proven to be a great grace as I learn to hone my own writing voice and share it with the world. I take none of your gifts to me for granted, *mil gracias!*

I extend my gratitude to the Claremont School of Theology, including (but not limited to!) the board of trustees: President Hagiya, Dean Dreitcer, and my wonderful faculty colleagues who supported my time away for writing. Special thanks go to Drs. Yohana Junker, Yuki Schwartz, Stephanie Butler, and Rev. Alecia Glaize, who were each so gracious to step in and fulfill my administrative duties so that I could take sabbatical time and engage the writing of this book. I am because we are.

Immense appreciation goes out to the Collegeville Institute and especially my wonderful cohort on "Mystic Activists," which was the first place I shared this manuscript publicly. Thanks to the wise leadership from Rev. Dr. Chanequa Walker Barnes and Rev. Jonathan Wilson-Hartgrove, along with the care and compassion from all the cohort members: Rev. Dr. Dietra Wise Baker,

Trauma and Renewal

Leonetta Elaiho, Dr. Gigi Khanyezi, Amanda Goldson, Rev. Laura Kigweba, Deanna Murshed, and Dr. Marcia Owens. Thank you to Carla Durand for your warm hospitality and coordination, which ensured we had a place of refuge, even in the middle of Minnesota! It was in the presence of this group I felt the courage and confidence to believe in this offering. *Si se puede!*

Thanks are due to the Louisville Institute and the many wonderful colleagues who engaged the initial idea of my book at the January seminary in Kentucky. It was only because of the generous book grant for scholars of color that I was enabled to take the needed time away for contemplation and writing. When I was unsure if this project was a good idea, having the LI community behind the book and affirm its importance in the world has been a powerful, life-affirming force. May this work and that of LI be divinely aligned, for such a time as this.

Lastly, I want to thank the divine presence that continues to be revealed to me in the quiet places of my soul. I am reminded that I am not alone and that I am loved. It is from a sense of belovedness that I humbly offer this book back unto the world so all life may flourish collectively and holistically. *Namaskaram.*

NOTES

INTRODUCTION

[1] I have previously written on the spiritual dimensions of my racialized experiences and how I understand identity formation related to social transformation in Aizaiah G. Yong, *Multiracial Cosmotheandrism: A Practical Theology of Multiracial Experiences* (Orbis, 2023).

[2] James Finley, "Transforming Trauma Recordings," James Finley (blog), https://jamesfinley.org/ish/.

[3] See my articles and book chapters on my contemplacostal identity and the ways it connects to trauma care in Aizaiah G. Yong, "Collective Despair and a Time for Emergence: Proposing a Contemplacostal Spirituality," *Religions* 15, no. 3 (2024): 349, https://doi.org/10.3390/rel15030349; Aizaiah G. Yong, "Cosmotheandric Eucharist, Contemplacostal Spirituality, and the Call to Relational Solidarity," in *Pentecostal Mission and Environmental Degradation*, ed. Amos Yong and Eugene Baron; Aizaiah G. Yong with Amos Yong, *The Inequitable Silencing of Many Tongues: A Critical and Pastoral Response to the Economic, Political, and Racialized Dimensions of the Pandemic in American Pentecostal-Charismaticism* (Langham Global, 2025).

[4] I have published numerous book chapters and journal articles on the "many tongues" of Pentecost; the foundational argument is laid out in Amos Yong, *The Spirit Poured Out on All Flesh: Pentecostalism and the Possibility of Global Theology* (Baker Academic, 2005).

Notes

5 I also see the oral tradition of testimony as a possible decolonial practice in connection to the peoples of the global majority who pass on wisdom primarily orally rather than through the written word.

6 Examples include Alexander Chow, *Chinese Public Theology: Generational Shifts and Confucian Imagination in Chinese Christianity* (Oxford University Press, 2018) and Chloë Starr, *Chinese Theology: Text and Context* (Yale University Press, 2016).

CHAPTER 1

1 See Shelly Rambo's theology of remaining as an important example of how trauma is something survivors live with for the entirety of their lives in *Spirit and Trauma: A Theology of Remaining* (Westminster John Knox Press, 2010).

2 "Trauma," American Psychological Association, last modified October 2023, https://www.apa.org/topics/trauma.

3 See Musa W. Dube, "African Eco-Feminisms: African Women Writing Earth, Gender and the Sacred," in *Ecofeminist Perspectives from African Women Creative Writers*, ed. Enna Sukutai Gudhlanga, Musa Wenkosi Dube, and Limakatso E. Pepenene (Springer International Publishing, 2024), 3–33, https://doi.org/10.1007/978-3-031-48509-1_1.

4 See Y. Golub et al., "Effects of In Utero Environment and Maternal Behavior on Neuroendocrine and Behavioral Alterations in a Mouse Model of Prenatal Trauma," *Developmental Neurobiology* 76, no. 11 (November 2016): 1254–65, https://doi.org/10.1002/dneu.22387.

5 For an initial autobiographical sketch, see Aizaiah G. Yong, "From Every Tribe, Language, People, and Nation: Diaspora,

Notes

Hybridity, and the Coming Reign of God," in *Global Diasporas and Mission*, ed. Chandler H. Im and Amos Yong, Regnum Edinburgh Centenary Series 23 (Regnum Books International, 2014), 253–61.

6 See Walter H. Slote, "Psychocultural Dynamics within the Confucian Family," in *Confucianism and the Family*, ed. Walter H. Slote and George A. DeVos (State University of New York Press, 1999), 37–51, esp. 41–43.

7 Consistent with this characterization, "The father is not supposed to be physically close to the son. Physical closeness seems to be a prerogative of mother and son. Nevertheless, the father remains intimate with the son as his constant companion"; Tu Wei-Ming, *Confucian Thought: Selfhood as Creative Transformation* (State University of New York Press, 1985), 124. I will return in a moment to the issue of intimacy referenced at the end.

8 Francis L. K. Hsu, "Confucianism in Comparative Context," in *Confucianism and the Family*, ed. Walter H. Slote and George A. DeVos (State University of New York Press, 1999), 53–71, at 63.

9 See Emma De Vynck, Heather Marie Boynton, and Victoria Frances Burns, "Pulled from the Shoreline in Search of Spacious Spirituality: Journeys of Spiritual Distress, Resilience, and Posttraumatic Growth for Women of Evangelical Christian Backgrounds in a Canadian Context," *Religions* 14, no. 9 (September 19, 2023): 1193, https://doi.org/10.3390/rel14091193.

10 See Baron Friedrich von Hügel, *The Mystical Element of Religion*: volumes 1 and 2 (J. M. Dent, 1909).

11 See where I recount many of these evidence-based studies, Aizaiah G. Yong, "Collective Despair and a Time for Emergence: Proposing a Contemplacostal Spirituality," *Religions* 15, no. 3 (March 13, 2024): 349, https://doi.org/10.3390/rel15030349.

Notes

12 See Irene Visser, "Decolonizing Trauma Theory: Retrospect and Prospects," *Humanities* 4, no. 2 (June 23, 2015): 250–65, https://doi.org/10.3390/h4020250.

13 See Fernando Montes Ruiz La Mascara De Piedra, *Simbolismo y Personalidad Aymaras en la Historia* (Editorial Armonia, 1999), 368.

14 See Tu Wei-ming, "Pain and Suffering in Confucian Self-Cultivation," *Philosophy East and West* 34, no. 4 (October 1984): 379, https://doi.org/10.2307/1399173.

15 Raimon Panikkar, for example, distinguishes pain as something inherent in physical life, sorrow as primarily psychological, and suffering as that which involves the physical, psychological, and the spiritual; see Raimon Panikkar, *The Experience of God: Icons of the Mystery* (Fortress Press, 2006), 105–106.

16 See Barbara Ann Holmes, *Crisis Contemplation: Healing the Wounded Village* (Center for Action and Contemplation, 2021), 57.

17 This is also affirmed by David McLain Carr. See David McLain Carr, *Holy Resilience: The Bible's Traumatic Origins* (Yale University Press, 2014).

18 See Shelly Rambo, *Resurrecting Wounds: Living in the Afterlife of Trauma* (Baylor University Press, 2017).

19 See James Finley, The Healing Path: A Memoir and an Invitation (Orbis Books, 2023), ix.

CHAPTER 2

1 Bessel A. van der Kolk, *The Body Keeps the Score: Brain, Mind, and Body in the Healing of Trauma* (Penguin, 2015).

2 Van der Kolk, *The Body Keeps the Score*, 82.

3 See Shelly Rambo's *Spirit and Trauma: A Theology of Remaining* (Westminster John Knox Press, 2010) where she discusses "resisting a linear time of healing" (130).

Notes

4 Barbara Holmes describes the effects of crisis and collective trauma as a "collective freefall" and a "welcoming darkness" when we are unsure about the direction we are headed, a direction that "shatters normalcy ... in liminal space." See Barbara Holmes, *Crisis Contemplation: Healing the Wounded Village* (Center for Action and Contemplation, 2021), 57, 128.

5 See Birgit Haehnel and Melanie Ulz, eds., *Slavery in Art and Literature: Approaches to Trauma, Memory, and Visuality*, Kulturwissenschaften (Frank & Timme, 2010), and Thomas Hubl, "Global Social Witnessing," The Pocket Project, accessed May 10, 2024, https://pocketproject.org/global-social-witnessing/.

6 John of the Cross and Kieran Kavanaugh, *St. John of the Cross: Selected Writings* (Paulist Press, 1987), 55.

7 See Howard Zehr and The Center for Peace and Justice Education, Villanova University, "The Intersection of Restorative Justice with Trauma Healing, Conflict Transformation and Peacebuilding," *Journal for Peace and Justice Studies* 18, no. 1 (2009): 20–30, https://doi.org/10.5840/peacejustice2009181/23.

8 See Kaira Jewel Lingo's "Touching the Earth: A Black Buddhist Perspective on Connecting with and Healing Ourselves and Our Ancestors," *Journal of Contemplative Inquiry* 9, no. 1 (2022): art. 16.

9 See Phyllis Jeffers-Coly, *We Got Soul, We Can Heal: Overcoming Racial Trauma through Leadership, Community and Resilience* (Toplight, 2022).

10 When first practicing this, it is important to select a situation that does not feel too activating. And if you find yourself unexpectedly activated or are accompanying someone who feels retraumatized in the moment, consider seeking professional help.

Notes

CHAPTER 3

1 See Howard Thurman and Walter E. Fluker, *The Papers of Howard Washington Thurman*, vol. 1: *My People Need Me, June 1918–March 1936* (University of South Carolina Press, 2009), 174.

2 Dalai Lama XIV Bstan-'dzin-rgya-mtsho et al., *Mission JOY: Finding Happiness in Troubled Times*, dir. Louie Psihoyos and Peggy Callahan (2021).

3 See Mark 15:34 and Matthew 27:46.

CHAPTER 4

1 I am thankful for Frank Rogers Jr. who helped to shape my thinking on the ways to discern how altered states of consciousness can be supportive to our spiritual lives, one of the main criteria being the fruit that comes from them, and how any experience supports us (or not) to live more fully engaged lives rather than distant or closed off.

2 Donna Schaper and Howard Thurman, eds., *40-Day Journey with Howard Thurman*, 40-Day Journey Series (Augsburg Books, 2009), 32.

3 While it would be impossible to write out all the details of my experience, my goal in presenting a summary of the vision here is to give readers an experiential taste of the experience and to see possibilities for personal, holistic, and collective integration.

4 See Robin L. Carhart-Harris's entropic brain hypothesis in Robin L. Carhart-Harris, "The Entropic Brain—Revisited," *Neuropharmacology* 142 (November 2018): 167–78, https://doi.org/10.1016/j.neuropharm.2018.03.010, which articulates how important it is for the brain to create new neural pathways de-stabilizing entrenched patterns.

Notes

5 See C. G. Jung, Richard Winston, and Clara Winston, *Memories, Dreams, Reflections*, ed. Aniela Jaffé (Fontana Press, 1995), 349–59.

6 See Thomas Merton, *Conjectures of a Guilty Bystander* (Image Books, 1989), 153.

7 See the story of Sitting Bull and other Indigenous Peoples who had visions and dreams in Ernest Thompson Seton, *The Gospel of the Redman* (Book Tree, 2006).

8 Alana Levandoski and James Finley, *Sanctuary: Exploring the Healing Path*, accessed February 13, 2023, https://cac.org/wp-content/uploads/2018/10/Sanctuary-songs-transcript.pdf.

9 The apostle Paul goes so far as to wish fellowship with Christ's sufferings as it conforms to Christ's death so that he may participate in Christ's resurrection (Philippians 3:10–11).

CHAPTER 5

1 See Aizaiah Yong, "Cosmotheandric Renewal: Exploring the Contemporary Relevance of the Yijing in North America" (CIRPIT Review, 2024).

2 See Raimon Panikkar, https://www.raimon-panikkar.org/english/gloss-ecosofi.html.

3 Vita Dutton Scudder, *Saint Catherine of Siena as Seen in Her Letters* (Kessinger Publishing, 2006), 295, https://mycatholic.life/saints/saints-of-the-liturgical-year/april-29-saint-catherine-of-siena-virgin-and-doctor-of-the-church/her-letters/.

Notes

CHAPTER 6

[1] Sharon Dodua Otoo, "For Those Who Have Been in Crisis," in Kerstin Schmidt and Joost Van Loon, eds., *Herausforderung Solidarität: Konzepte—Kontroversen—Perspektiven, vol. 10, K'Universale—Interdisziplinäre Diskurse zu Fragen der Zeit* (Transcript Verlag, 2024), 29, https://doi.org/10.14361/9783839461013.

[2] Thomas Merton, *New Seeds of Contemplation* (Shambhala, 2003), 297.

[3] Yvette Flunder, *Where the Edge Gathers: Building a Community of Radical Inclusion* (Pilgrim Press, 2005), 25–26.

CHAPTER 7

[1] It is interesting to note that experimental psychologists have long been studying the importance of religion, spirituality, and ritual as they relate to individual and social benefits. See, for example, the work of Miguel Farias, in "The Force of Rituals: Social and Psychobiological Processes" (Psychology Engaged Cross-Training Programme, University of Birmingham, July 29, 2024), where he shows how religious rituals are supported through multiple circles of community.

[2] I asked each of the three their names when I first met them, though I change their names here to keep anonymity.

[3] Substance Abuse and Mental Health Services Administration. (2024). Results from the 2023 National Survey on Drug Use and Health: Mental Health Detailed Tables.

[4] Substance Abuse and Mental Health Services Administration, "Key Substance Use and Mental Health Indicators in the United States: Results from the 2021 National Survey on Drug

Notes

Use and Health" (HHS Publication No. PEP22-07-01-005, NSDUH Series H-57) (2022), https://www.samhsa.gov/data/report/2021-nsduh-annual-national-report.

CHAPTER 8

[1] Julian of Norwich, *The Showings: Uncovering the Face of the Feminine in Revelations of Divine Love*, trans. Mirabai Starr (Hampton Roads, 2022), foreword by Richard Rohr.

[2] I make a point to name this as colonial Christianity because even within the broad Christian tradition, there have been practices of honoring ancestors, although used often in the language of "saints."